RABBI YEHUDA ASHLAG

AN
ENTRANCE
TO THE
ZOHAR

Compiled and Edited by
DR. PHILIP S. BERG

THE KEY TO THE PORTALS OF
JEWISH MYSTICISM

Published by the Press of the "Research Centre of Kabbalah" for the
Dissemination of the Study of Kabbalah

THE OLD CITY JERUSALEM, ISRAEL

To My Wife Tova

THE PUBLICATION OF THIS VOLUME
HAS BEEN MADE POSSIBLE THROUGH
THE GENEROUS SUPPORT OF
THE FOLLOWING

מר ומרת מוריס שינקר

MR. & MRS. MORRIS SHENKER
St. Louis, Missouri

DEDICATED TO THE MEMORY OF
HIS FATHER

AVRAHAM ABA SHENKER ע"ה

Mr. & Mrs. Morrie Yohai
Kings Point, New York

Dr. Norman E. Frimer
Bklyn, N.Y.

Mr. Harold Kasimow
Grinnell, Iowa

Mr. E. Christiansen
Spenard. Alaska

Arlene G. Fitzpatrick
Medford, Mass.

Mr. Norman Mailer
Bklyn, N.Y.

Mr. & Mrs. David Weiss
South Branch, N.J.

Dr. & Mrs. Jack Harris
Massapequa, L.I., N.Y.

Ira & Natalie Silverman
West Hempstead, N.Y.

The Kehiath Jeshurun
Rabbi Joseph Lookstein
New York, N.Y.

Mr. Irving Super
Bklyn, N.Y.

Rabbi Judah Nadich
New York, N.Y.

Mr. David A. Jackson
Chicago, Ill.

Mr. B. G. Greenblatt
Teaneck, N.J.

Mr. Samuel S. Goldstein
New York, N.Y.

Dr. Victor Kassel
Salt Lake City, Utah

[iv]

Mr. Robert Z. Kaplan
Toledo, Ohio

Mr. James H. Headen
Point Richmond, Calif.

Dr. & Mrs. Paul Flicker
Sommerville, N.J.

Mr. Benjamin Koenigsberg
New York, N.Y.

Mr. Louis Kahan
Tulsa, Okla.

Mr. James Marshall
New York, N.Y.

Mr. Donald Bloxsom
Los Angeles, Calif.

Ms. Jimmilee Farmer
Camdenton, Missouri

RABBI YEHUDA ASHLAG'S PUBLICATIONS

Twenty-one volume translation — commentary on the entire Zohar

■

Sixteen volume textbook on the
Ten Luminous Emanations of the Ari-Rabbi Isaac Luria

■

Panim Meirot Upanim Masbirot — Four volume advanced textbook
on the Etz Chaim

■

Four introductions to various branches of Kabbalah

■

Bet Shaar L'kavonot — on prayer

■

Ha'Ilon Ha'Kodosh — A visual aid with diagrams revealing the
process of emanation and evolution

■

ACKNOWLEDGMENTS

I wish to express my appreciation to Rabbi Mordechai Klein for his assistance in the translation. Grateful acknowledgment is extended to my friend Morrie Yohai for his beneficial suggestions and kind helpfulness at every stage in the publication of this volume.

TABLE OF CONTENTS

PART TWO

AN INTRODUCTION TO THE ZOHAR

PREFACE

The year was 1955, the date, the Holy of Holy days, Yom Kippur, and the concealed light of the most profound mystic of our generation shined as it had never shone in its corporeal form. The soul of Rabbi Yehuda Ashlag, of Blessed Memory, elevated to a union with the Absolute. The world below would sound no mourning bells nor eulogies expressed. The magnificient truths and paths of light that his pen created would have to wait until such time as a spiritual revival would engulf the masses.

However, having the unflinching faith that the truths of Kabbalah together with the Ashlagian approach to its under standing will ultimately prevail, then it is a source of gratitude that the first and comprehensive introduction to the Zohar has now appeared in English. This will permit the earnest student of the Zohar an understanding of its abstruse and complex text, without which, there might have remained a perpetual obscurity to its knowledge. *Never before* has a complete *translation* of the *entire Zohar* appeared. While commentaries have been written by famed Kabbalists which provided the necessary keys in comprehending the Zohar, nevertheless, the difficulty in understanding these works prevented a thorough comprehension. Additionally, they did not provide a page-by-page explanation of the Zohar which might have facilitated the widespread interest and readership of this sublime text and avoided the confusion and misunderstanding which subsequently surrounded this basic text of the Kabbalah, the Zohar.

Consequently, this introduction will prepare the student with proper guidelines, fundamental rules correlating the general principles contained in the text, deçined limits to which the Zohar does or does not allude to, and finally the unraveling of its mystical terminology. When a mastery of this introduction will have been achieved, the individual will then find the portals to the Zohar unlocked. The translation and meticulous commentary on *each* section of the Zohar by Rabbi Ashlag *will* provide the necessary tools so sorely needed in its comprehension.

At the close of the nineteenth century, the spirit of Kabbalah which had been revived centuries earlier, was all but dead, and would not be rekindled until such time as a translation and commentary on the entire Zohar based on a comprehensive understanding of the Lurianic system would be made available.

In the midst of considerable opposition by the Talmudist towards Kabbalah, there appeared a mystic and Kabbalist whose goal was to make the Kabbalah accessible to all whose *desire* was for an understanding of these sublime and esoteric teachings. This Kabbalist's name was Rabbi Yehuda Ashlag (1886-1955). His voluminous works would finally lay to rest the unfounded fears of Talmudic authorities that the Kabbalah was not a topic of general study and that only the select were permitted entrance to its secret wisdom. For those already spiritually oriented in their search to experience the Divine, for those whose needs could not be satisfied with traditional views and established dogma in their approach to the performing of the Mitzvot (the commandments of the Torah), for the scientist on a collision course with spirituality, they now could find renewed strength and knowledge within Kabbalah. Rabbi Ashlag presented a new dimension to an existing religion, where established religious practices have been failing, where rituals of the Torah were considered primarily rites of tradition and remembrance, similarly to the holidays celebrated by many nations throughout the world in observance of their attaining freedom and liberty. The need for a new perspective within Judaism rapidly became apparent. The continuous decline of interest in Judaism and its rejection required a re-evaluation of our spiritual heritage, towards which Rabbi Ashlag directed himself. It was through the comprehension of the Kabbalah and a living experience within the framework of Judaism, that a more meaningful religious experience would result. He opened the doors to spiritual Judaism recognizing that no precept was to be performed for the purpose of remembrance or tradition alone, but rather as an experience that necessarily must and would provide a spiritual "high" for the individual himself. It was through these rituals, that an individual reenacted the exact scene that had once taken place where a significant flow of spirituality or light had emanated from the Divine Being. Since spirituality transcends time, space and motion, one may reconstruct the mystical dimension of a scene that may well have taken place thousands of years ago, by projecting oneself into the past by employing the tools provided in the Torah. Thus one becomes rejuvenated and recharged with a spiritual vitality to sustain him through difficult and sometimes overwhelming forces. Negating the viewpoint of "religious obligation" as the reason for performing the rituals, Rabbi Ashlag had only to refer to Rabbi Shimon Bar Yohai discussing ritual and precepts in the Zohar, "Prayer and ritual devoid of meaning and spirituality are similar to straw, the epitomy of lifelessness". Religion does not permeate the structure of our society because of its inability to fulfill the spiritual needs of the individual. "If these needs are not met" remarked Rabbi Ashlag "then we may expect a totally despiritualized and demoralized society, the likes of which has never been experienced in the history of mankind.

Known as the pioneer of modern Kabbalism, Rabbi Ashlag developed a new approach and path to understanding the Lurianic system, which was revealed in his sixteen volume textbook called "The Study of the Ten Luminous Emanations". The *Eser Sefirot* or Ten Luminous Emanations and its corresponding interpretation by the *Ari*, Rabbi Isaac Luria, serves as the fundamental element encompassing all of the principles of Kabbalah. Consequently, before one becomes proficient in the wisdom of Kabbalah, a thorough knowledge and comprehension of the *Eser Sefirot* is necessary, without which Jewish mysticism might very well remain a mystery, beyond the grasp of the masses.

In this work, a logical and intellectual system was devised which was capable of transmitting the essence of the transcendent realm by utilizing an array of symbols and illustrations which he felt would best describe what was beyond physical perception. His "Ten Luminous Emanations" dealt with those concepts which for centuries have eluded even the dedicated scholar. Heretofore, the student of Kabbalah could not expect to come close to a full comprehension of the intricate Lurianic system. The intimate relationships between the physical and metaphysical are presented together with a connected series of evolutions to this present world. A detailed presentation of the relationships surrounding the Creator and creative beings, coupled with a complete outline of the basic doctrines of Kabbalah, is included in this work. This has achieved for man a method together with specific guidelines which will enable the individual to achieve a greater awareness of himself and his level of consciousness.

In addition to his "Ten Luminous Emanations", Rabbi Ashlags' massive and monumental work on the entire Zohar would leave an indelible imprint on Judaic scholarship and far more important, the turning point in our attempt to unravel the mysteries of the Zohar.

This was the very first translation of the *entire* Zohar into modern Hebrew ever to appear and would now permit the student to delve into any portion of its content. Realizing that a comprehensive translation would not suffice for the reader, he successfully completed his commentary on the difficult passages of the Zohar which have constantly eluded the searching student. It is through this commentary, utilizing the system of Rabbi Luria's Ten *Sefirot*, that the once abstruse Zohar couched in difficult Aramaic language, became intelligible. Rather than dealing with effects as our scientific society has become accustomed to, the revelation of *root cause and reason* now became accessible.

In addition to this feat he organized the Zohar to make it more readable and easier to study. He divided it into paragraphs and sections to indicate the various topical discussions. Heretofore, the Zohar had appeared as one continuous paragraph. Now on *each page* one would find a topical caption to indicate quickly the subject matter discussed. Source references were made available to permit the student to find the passages quoted in the Bible. Realizing that printed material was constantly subjected to errors by the printer, he made corrections where he understood a mistake had appeared. In recognizing the criticism that these corrections might evoke, he listed every available reference which differed from his own version to permit the student the choice of words that the student himself might determine to be the proper insertion. The student would now find on *each page* topical captions indicating the material discussed, together with a page reference to the original Zoharic text. A list of abbreviations was also made available to avoid any confusion that might arise from the original text. To further facilitate the accessibility to this work on mysticism, he constructed an index which permitted the student to find any particular subject that was of interest. Included in his edition were other commentaries which he felt would be a useful tool in understanding some of the more difficult passages. This work finally appeared in 21 volumes, and if translated into English by the Research Centre would fill some 150 volumes.

Now the humanist, philosopher, jurist, astronomer, astrologer, physician, metallurgist, psychiatrist, and individuals within *all* fields of scientific endeavors (not to mention the communications field including extra-sensory-perception, the ultimate in restoring world-harmony) all would now benefit and learn basic and root knowledge to supplement the existing information already available in their particular field of knowledge. "The dawn of a new tomorrow with greater expectations for the future can and will be realized". Rabbi Ashlag remarked, "if we merely heed the beneficial advice of

Rabbi Shimon Bar Yohai" as he stated "through the medium of this Book (the Zohar) will Israel and the world merit the final redemption" (Zohar Naso., p. 124).

To obtain a better insight into the character of this gifted and interesting Kabbalist, the likes of whom has not been known since the golden era of the Ari Hakodesh, Rabbi Isaac Luria, I refer to a letter dated the third day of Teveth, in the year 5688 (1928) written by the author to an uncle of his:

"On the 12th day of Cheshvan, Friday morning came an individual who revealed himself as one *completely* knowledgeable in the Wisdom of the Kabbalah as well as in all other forms of wisdom. At the very outset, I sensed the Divine wisdom adorning him and his words disclosing profound and beautiful concepts. I, in the main, remained unaffected. He subsequently assured me that he would reveal to me the Wisdom of the Kabbalah in its entirety and we continued a study session for three months, each evening after 12 midnight at his home. After continued insistence that he reveal the *inner* mysteries of the Kabbalah, he finally consented. The resulting "limitless high" of that revelation, the supreme degree of joy was beyond description. From that moment on I began to acquire an element of ego-centricity, the garment of pride. As this powerful feeling steadily increased, the separation between my master and I became incessantly greater, a factor which I completely failed to recognize. This continued for several days at which point I no longer found my master awaiting me at our appointed rendezvous. I then realized that he had in fact severed our spiritual ties and consequently I began to mend my ways, wrap myself in a cloak of humility.

On the morning of the ninth of Nissan I again met my

master and begged forgiveness for my behaviour, and our relationship resumed as it had been in the past. He then revealed a *Sod* (secret or inner meaning) concerning Mikveh (Ritual Immersion) exploring the very essence of life, where the most mysterious enigmas of life are disclosed. This brought on an ecstacy of such proportions literally creating a total *Devekut* (cleaving to Divine Essence), completely separating from corporeality and tearing assunder the veil of eternal life.

I then noticed a gradual physical weakening of the master and I did not leave his home. The following day, the tenth day of Nissan, in the year עטר"ת, 5679 (1919), he departed to the everlasting world above.

As a result of my loss, the cup of agony was filled to overflowing, hopelessly languishing with a despairing heart. The pain was indescribable and a bitter one. My heart, which had been so full of expectations, yearning to merit one day the hidden and unfathomed depths of the Kabbalah, was now broken. I remained as a one stranded, weak and stumbling, void of anything and everything. Because of my extreme sorrow, the profound knowledge that I obtained from him temporarily vanished. From that period on, my eyes focused to the Worlds on High, lamenting with despair to no end. This state of mind did not cease for a single moment until I again found favor in the eyes of my Creator, Blessed Be He, and together with the merit of my Sainted Teacher and his Torah stood by me, whereupon the fountains of heavenly wisdom suddenly burst forth to a welcome heart, as a flowing well. With the grace of the Almighty, I remembered all of the mysteries received from my master, of Blessed Memory.

How can I, so base and unlettered find praise of the

Almighty. For from the very outset, the Creator has known of my affliction, having no intelligence nor comprehension to praise Him for this continuous beneficience and ceaseless out-pouring of His abundance. But, then who am I to say or direct His motives or actions.

My Sainted Teacher, of Blessed Memory, was known throughout the city as a trustworthy and accomplished businessman. However, his knowledge of the Kabbalah remained completely obscured, and I was prohibited from ever revealing his name''.

Were it not for his revealing works on the Kabbalah, one might be unwilling to accept or take note of the preceding mystical letter. However, his massive literary legacy, will stand as a moving testimonial, that at long last, the Creator with his never ending mercy, has finally revealed simplicity in the esoteric wisdom of the Kabbalah through his trusted servant, Rabbi Yehuda Ashlag. Hopefully, this approach will be the forerunner of a new mystical revival and spiritual awakening in Judaism. The bright memory of the Sainted Tanna Rabbi Shimon Bar Yohai illumined with the Book of Splendor, the Zohar, shall ultimately remove the melancholy period of strife and hatred, then truth and peace shall forever prevail.

Dr. Philip S. Berg

PART ONE

A PREFACE TO THE ZOHAR

CHAPTER 1

QUESTIONS RELATING TO ESSENCE

In this introduction I will be attempting to clarify some matters which at first sight seem simple and obvious. By this I mean that everybody is familiar with these matters, and indeed a tremendous amount of ink has been used in the various attempts to clarify them. Yet despite all this, we still have not reached a sufficient and clear understanding of them. We still have to find answers for the following questions:

1. What is the essence of our being?
2. What is our role in the long chain of existence of which we are but a very small link?
3. Self-reflection reveals to us our imperfections and our lowly position. Yet, how is this possible, seeing that we have been created by the Holy One, whose perfect agency must necessarily produce perfect works?
4. An accepted assumption is that the Creator is Good, and does good. Then why did He create so many beings whose entire existence consists of endless torture and suffering? Is it not to be expected that the good will do good, or at least not so much bad?
5. How is it possible that from the Eternal, Who has no beginning nor end, there should come forth finite perishable beings?

In order to fully understand all this, we must first engage in certain inquiries. Not in those areas where it is forbidden,* such as in the case of the Essence of the Almighty Creator, for no thought can encompass Him, therefore there is no way at all that we can think or speak about Him. But we shall direct our inquiries to His deeds as we are commanded to by the Torah: "Know the God of your father and serve Him." And as we find in the Hymn of Unity: "It is from Your deeds that we know You."

Our first inquiry is directed towards understanding how the creation can be conceived by us as being something entirely "new", meaning by that, a "new" thing which was not contained in the Almighty before He created it. It must be obvious to every understanding person that there is not a thing that was not contained in Him. Pure reason demands this assumption, for can someone give away what he does not possess?

Our second inquiry follows from this. If we were to assume that He is so Omnipotent that He can create something from nothing; something totally "new" which had absolutely no existence at all in Him, the question that must be asked then is: What is this existence that has no place at all within Him, but is completely new?

Our third inquiry is directed towards the saying by the Masters of Kabbalah that the soul (*Neshamah*) of a man is a part of God on high. By this they meant that there is no difference between Him and between the soul, except that He is the "whole" and the soul is a "part". They compared

---

* "Forbidden" is a term used to denote incomprehension, similarly to a man born blind comprehending the concept of light.

it to a stone that is cut away from a mountain. For there is no difference between the stone and the mountain, except that one is the "whole" and the other is a "part". Now the stone is separated from the mountain by a suitable implement and in this way the "part" becomes separate from the "whole". But how can one conceive of the Almighty separating a "part" of His Essence which would then become a "part" that was separate from Him, which means that the Soul can only be conceived of as being a "part" of His Essence?

The fourth inquiry is as follows. Since the Chariot of the Other Side (Evil Forces), and the "Shells" (*Kelipot*) are so utterly remote from His Holiness, to the extent that we cannot even envisage the distance, how is it possible that they should proceed from and exist through His Holiness, or even that His Holiness should actually be giving them their existence?

The fifth inquiry concerns the Resurrection of the dead. Since the physical body is such a contemptible thing, for from the very moment of its birth it is condemned to die and be buried. The Zohar even says that before the physical body has become completely decomposed and as long as even the slightest part of it still remains, the Soul (*Neshamah*) cannot ascend to its proper place in Paradise. Why then should it be necessary for it to rise again at the time of the Resurrection of the dead? Could the Holy One, Blessed be He, not give the Souls their fill of pleasure without the physical bodies being present? And even more amazing than this is the saying of our Sages of blessed memory "When the dead will be brought back to life they will be resurrected with all their infirmities, so that no-one will be able to say 'He is not the same!', and only afterwards will He cure their infirmities." We have to understand why it should matter to the Holy One, Blessed be He, that it might be said that they are not the same, to the extent that He should have to create them again with all their infirmities and then afterwards have to heal them.

The sixth inquiry concerns the Saying of the Sages that man is the centre of all existence; that all the Higher Worlds and also this material world were created for his sake. (*Zohar, Vayikra*: 48). And they even made it a man's duty to believe that it was just for his sake that the world was created (*Sanhedrin* 37a). Now on the face of it , it is not easy to understand why the Holy One, Blessed be He, should take so much trouble to create all this for such an insignificant human being whose worth when weighed against the worth of the existence of this material world is not even equivalent to that of a single hair, let alone when weighed against the worth of the Higher worlds which are infinite, and whose *exaltedness has no limits*? Furthermore, what need has a man for all this?

CHAPTER 2

PURPOSE OF CREATION

The best way of understanding all these questions and inquiries would be to consider the ultimate objective of the action, I mean by that, the purpose of the Creation. For it is impossible to understand anything while it is still being made, but only after it has been completed. It is quite obvious we are not dealing here with actions that were committed without any purpose, for only unbalanced minds act without any purpose. Now I know that there are some would-be scholars, who have thrown off the yoke of the Torah and of its Commandments, who claim that the Creator created the world and then abandoned it to its fate. The reason for this, they say, is that it does not befit the Creator in all His Exaltedness, to watch over their petty and despicable ways. However, the claim that they put forward is not based on knowledge, for it is not possible to decide that we are base and worthless unless we decide that it is we who created our own selves together with all these imperfect and despicable characteristics that we possess. But when we decide that the Almighty Creator, in His Supreme Perfection, is the craftsman who created and designed our bodies with all their good and bad tendencies, then it follows that no bad or contemptible or imperfect work could ever leave the hands of a perfect craftsman, but rather every single piece of work will be evidence of the high quality of its maker. Is it the fault of a ruined coat if it has been made by an inept tailor? A similar idea is expressed in a story related in the Talmud (*Ta'anit*, 20): "It happened once that Rabbi Eliezer, son of Rabbi Shimon, met by chance a man who was extremely ugly... and he said to him: 'How ugly this man is!'... He replied 'Go and say to the craftsman who made me: How ugly is this vessel which You have made!'."

Therefore those would-be scholars who say that because of our baseness and worthlessness, it does not befit the Almighty to watch over us and so He has abandoned us, are merely proclaiming their own ignorance. Imagine meeting a man to whom it had occurred to create creatures with the intention at the very outset that they should be tortured and made to suffer all their lives just like us, and then after that he decided to fling them behind his back without any desire at all to watch over them, or help them even a little. How deeply would you censure and despise him! Is it then possible to conceive of such an idea applying to the Almighty Who brought all being into existence?

Common sense demands that we should understand the opposite of what is superficially apparent. And we should decide that we are really such good and exalted creatures that there is no limit to our importance, which is exactly as befits the craftsman who made us. For all the short-comings and defects that you may care to think up about our bodies, even after you have answered them all away, are still only to be related to their Creator who created us together with all our inherent natural characteristics. It is clear that it is He who made us and not we ourselves, and that He also knew of all the consequences which would continue to result from all the characteristics and evil tendencies that He implanted in us. However, as we have said, we must look at the ultimate objective of the action, and then we will be able to understand everything. There is a well-known proverb that goes "Do not show a fool a job half-done".

Our Sages of blessed memory taught us (Etz Hayyim, the section on vessels, at the beginning of the first chapter), that the Holy One, Blessed be He, created the world only to give pleasure to those whom He created. So it is in this direction that we should concentrate all our attention, for this is the ultimate intention and purpose of the creation of the universe. Consider this: since the Thought of Creation was to give pleasure to those whom He created, it follows that He created within the Souls a very large measure of the "will to receive" that which He thought to give them. For the amount of any enjoyment and pleasure is measured by the amount of the "will to receive" them. The greater the "will to receive" is, the greater the pleasure will be, and the less the "will to receive" is, the amount of pleasure taken in receiving will also be proportionately less. And so the actual Thought of Creation necessarily requires the creation within the Souls (*Neshamot*) of an extremely large amount of the "will to receive" which would be appropriate for the large amount of pleasure which the Almighty thought of giving to the Souls. For tremendous enjoyment and a large "will to receive" go hand in hand.

When we know this, we will then be able to fully understand our second inquiry. We wanted to know what there was that did not exist at all in the Essence of the Almighty, but could be called a completely "new" creation of something from something non-existent. But now we know quite clearly that God's Thought of Creation, whose whole purpose was to give enjoyment to those He created, created out of necessity the "will to receive" from Him all the goodness and pleasantness that He thought for them. Obviously this "will to receive" was not contained in the Essence of the Almighty before He created it in the souls, for from whom could He have received anything? Therefore He created something completely "new" that was not contained within Him. In addition to this, it is clear that in accordance with the Thought of Creation there was no need at all to actually *create* more than this "will to receive", for this "new" creation was sufficient means through which the Almighty could fulfil the entire Thought of Creation, which was to give us enjoyment. All that was contained in the Thought of Creation, namely all those benefits that He thought for us, proceed directly from the Essence of the Almighty, therefore there is no need at all to create them anew, since they proceed as substances created from other substances already in existence, to the large "will to receive" that is within the soul. It should now be absolutely clear to us that the "will to receive" was the only substance in the entire creation, from beginning to end, that was actually created as something new.

CHAPTER 3

SIMILARITY AND DIFFERENCE OF FORM

This now leads us to a proper understanding of the words of the Masters of the Kabbalah that we mentioned in our third inquiry. We wondered how one could possibly say that the soul is a "part" of God on high, just like a stone that is cut out of the mountain, the only difference between them being that one is a "part" while the other is the "whole". We queried this analogy, because although we can accept this reasoning in the case of a stone that is cut out of the mountain — which then becomes a "part" of it by means of the appropriate implement, how can one possibly say this concerning the Essence of the Almighty? What was used to separate the Souls (*Neshamot*) from the Essence of the Almighty so that they should no longer be a part of the Creator but become something created?

In the light of what we have previously explained, this should all become perfectly understandable. For just as a blade slices and separates material things and divides them into two parts, so in the same way a "difference of form" separates spiritual substances and divides them into two parts. Let us use an example to make this clearer. When two people love each other you would say that they are so attached to each other that they have become just like one body. Whereas when two people hate each other, you would say that they are

— 19 —

as distant from each other as west is from east. Yet nearness or distance of place is not what is meant here, but rather it is the "similarity of form" that is intended. For when they are equal in form to each other, that is to say that he loves whatever his friend loves and he hates whatever his friend hates, then they love each other and are closely attached to each other. But if there is some difference between them, he loves a certain thing even though his friend hates that thing, then they can be said to hate each other and be distant from each other in proportion to that amount of "difference of form" that exists between them. So if, for example, they are complete opposites, everything that one loves is hated by the other, and everything that he hates is loved by the other, then they are as distant from each other as east is from west, they are poles apart.

So you will find that in spiritual matters, "difference of form" works in the same way that a blade separates material substances. The distance between the two will be in proportion to how opposite in form they are to each other. Now you will understand from this that since there is implanted in the Souls, the "will to receive" His pleasure, which is not to be found at all in the Creator (for from whom could He receive anything?,) then this "difference of form" which the Souls possess acts to separate them from the Essence of the Almighty like a blade cuts out a stone from a mountain. It was by means of this "difference of form" that the Souls were detached from the Creator and became separate from Him, so that they became something that was created. However, whatever a Soul (*Neshamah*) possesses of the light of the Almighty is derived from existent matter that was already existent as part of the Essence of the Almighty. Therefore with regard to the light that a Soul receives into its' vessel (which vessel is the "will to receive"), there is absolutely no difference between it and the Essence of the Almighty. For the light comes to it directly from the Essence of the Almighty as existent from existent. The only difference between the Souls (*Neshamot*) and the Essence of the Almighty is that the Souls are a "part" of the Essence of the Almighty. That is to say, that the light a Soul receives into its vessel, which is the "will to receive", becomes a "part" that is *separate* from God, since it is contained within the "different form" of the "will to receive". It is this "difference of form" that make it into a "part", and it was through this that the Souls became detached from the "whole" and became a "part". The only difference between them is that one is the "whole" and the other is a "part", just like a stone that is cut from a mountain. You should reflect well on this, for it is not possible to go in fuller length into this matter in this introduction.

CHAPTER 4

SYSTEMS OF HOLINESS AND UNCLEANNESS

An opening has now been made that will enable us to reach an understanding of the fourth inquiry. This was, how is it possible that the Chariot of Uncleanness and the "Shells" (*Kelipot*) were formed from the Holiness of the Almighty, seeing that they are really very distant from His Holiness? And why does He then sustain them and preserve them? To understand this, one must first understand what the whole existence of Uncleanliness and of the "Shells" is all about. You should know that this large "will to receive", which we already described as being the essence of the Souls from the aspect of their having been 'created' to receive all that was contained in the Thought of Creation, will not always remain in its original form in the Souls. For if it did, the Souls would then be condemned to be eternally separated from the Almighty, since it is the "difference of form" that the Souls possess that keeps them apart from Him. So it was in order to repair this matter of separation that is an integral aspect of the vessels of the souls, that the Almighty created all the worlds. He then divided them up into two systems, according to the 'mystery' of "one parallel to the other God made them";* on the one hand the four worlds

---

* Talmud Hagigah P. 15a

of Emanation, Creation, Formation and Action of Holiness, and parallel to them the four worlds of Emanation, Creation, Formation and Action of Uncleanness. He implanted the "will to impart" in the system of the worlds of Emanation, Creation, Formation and Action of Holiness, and He removed from these the "will to receive" for one's own self (as is described elsewhere in my Introduction to the Wisdom of the Kabbalah, 14-19), and He placed it into the system of the worlds of Emanation, Creation, Formation and Action of Uncleanness, and because of it they became separated from the Creator and from all the worlds of Holiness. It was for this reason that the "Shells" are called "dead" as in "The offerings of the dead",* and the wicked who are drawn to them are also called by the same name. As our Sages of blessed memory said "Wicked men even during their lifetime are called dead".** For the "will to receive" that is implanted in them in a form that is completely opposite to the Holiness of the Almighty, separates them from the life of the living, and they are poles apart from Him. For the Almighty has nothing at all to do with "receiving" but only with "imparting", whereas the "Shells" (*Klippot*) have nothing at all to do with "imparting" but only with receiving for their own enjoyment, and there is no opposite greater than this. You have already learned that spiritual distance begins with just a slight "difference of form", but it ends with a complete "opposite of form" which is where the distance ends on the lowest rank.

---

* (Psalms 106:28).
** Talmud Berachot P. 18b

Then after the creation of the two systems, the worlds evolved until the existence of this material world, where there is to be found a physical body as well as a Soul — (*Neshama*), also time for "ruin", for correction and repair (*Tikun*). The physical body is actually the "will to receive" which extends from the root of the Thought of the Creation, as we explained previously, and passes through the system of the worlds of Uncleanness, as it is written "Man was born a wild donkey".* He then remains in the grips of that world until his thirteenth year. This period is his time of "ruin".

Through his occupying himself with the *Mitzvot*** (God's commandments) from the time he becomes thirteen years old, which he does in order to give pleasure to his Creator, he begins to purify the "will to receive" for himself that is implanted in him, and he gradually transforms it into imparting to others. For it is through this, that the holy soul that has its roots in the Thought of Creation proceeds. Then it passes through the systems of the worlds of holiness, where it becomes clothed with a physical body. This is the time of the "correction" (*Tikun*). It thus proceeds to acquire and achieve to the levels of the holiness of the Thought of Creation that is in the Blessed "Endless". These help a man to transform the "will to receive" for himself alone, that he has in him, to "receiving for the sake of imparting" pleasure to

---

* Job, 11:12
** Mitzvot are the conditioning systems which enable man to prepare one's own vessel or "receiving set" with the maximum capacity to "tune in" to the Light which is constantly transmitted by the root source, namely, the Creator. Prayers and other precepts are the cables through which one may "tune in" with proper meditation. These cables (prayer and precepts) without proper understanding and Kavanot (Meditation) is similar to an electric cable without current.

his Creator and not for his own personal benefit. It is in this way that a man acquires a "similarity of form" to his Creator, for "receiving in order to impart" is considered to be pure imparting. (One can see an example of this in the Talmud, (*Kiddushim* 7a) that in the case of a woman marrying an important man, if she gives him money and he says the words of betrothal, she is betrothed. For although she is supposed to receive the money, his receiving it in order to give pleasure to the woman that is giving it to him is considered imparting as though he had actually given to her). By this means a man acquires a complete attachment to the Almighty, for spiritual attachment is none other than "similarity of form". (As our Sages wrote: "How is it possible to become attached to the Almighty? But rather become attached to His characteristics").* It is through this that a man becomes worthy of receiving all the good, pleasantness and gentleness that is in the Thought of Creation.

You should now understand the whole matter of the 'correction' (*Tikun*) of the "will to receive" that was implanted in the Souls by the Thought of the Creation. The Creator prepared for them the two parallel systems through which the Souls pass and become divided into two aspects, the physical body and the Soul (*Nefesh*) which are wrapped around each other. It is through Torah and *Mitzvot* that they finally transform the "will to receive" to become like the "will to impart". When that happens they will be able to receive all the good that is in the Thought of Creation. Then they will achieve a very strong attachment to the Almighty in conse-

---

* Talmud Ketubot, P. 111a

quence of their having achieved, by means of their working at Torah and *Mitzvot*, a "similarity of form" to their Creator. This is the final state of "correction" (*Tikun*). Then, since there will no longer be any need for the Unclean Side (Evil Forces), these will be consumed from the earth and "death will be swallowed up for all eternity". Thus the constant work at the Torah and at the *Mitzvot* that have been given to the entire world for a period of six thousand years which constitute a world, and to a single individual for the period of the seventy years of his life, exists only to bring them to the state of complete "correction" which will bring them to the "similarity in form". The whole existence of the systems of the "Shells" and of Uncleanness, and of their derivation from the Holiness of the Almighty, should now be understood as being absolutely necessary for the continued creation of physical bodies which will afterwards be corrected by Torah and *Mitzvot*. If these physical bodies, with the defective "will to receive" that they contain, did not come to us through the system of Uncleanness, it would never be possible for us to correct them, for a man cannot correct what he does not possess.

However, the following question has not yet been answered. How is it that the "will to receive", which is so imperfect and defective, should come to be in the Thought of Creation of the "Endless", Blessed be He, whose unity cannot be explained by any word or thought? The explanation is as follows: In reality, as soon as there was a Thought to Create the souls, His Thought completed it all, for the Almighty does not have any need of implements like we do, but all the Souls and all the worlds that were to be created full of all kinds of goodness and pleasure and gentleness that He thought for them, came immediately into existence together with the final perfection that the Souls attain at the end of their "correction": (that is to say, after the "will to receive" that is in all Souls has been fully corrected, and this "will" has then become transformed into pure "imparting" to the Almighty Emanator). The reason for this is that in the Eternity of the Almighty, past, present and future go together, and the future is also part of the present. The whole dimension of time and the restrictions caused by it have no relevance for the Almighty (c.f. *Zohar* on *Mishpatim* 51. Also *Zohar Hadash*, page 3). For this reason the whole defective "will to receive" was never in its "form of separation" part of the "Endless", Blessed be He, but on the contrary that "similarity of form" that will eventually become manifest at the end of the "correction", became manifest immediately in the Eternity of the Almighty. It was in accordance with the 'secret'* (*Sod*) that our Sages of blessed memory said (in The Perkei de Rabbi Eliezer): Before the world was created, He and His Name were One, for the 'form of separation' that is contained in the "will to receive" never appeared in the state of the Souls that came into existence through the Thought of Creation, but rather they were closely attached to Him by a "similarity of form" accordings to the 'mystery' of He and His Name are One. (See further the first chapter of my book Ten Luminous Emanations: vol. 1).

---

* The Hebrew word Sod is translated as secret. In Kabbalah it is better defined as inner or hidden meaning.

CHAPTER 5

THREE PHASES OF THE SOUL

Accordingly, we necessarily find that the Souls generally go through three Phases. The first Phase is when they are to be found in the Blessed "Endless" in the Thought of Creation where they already have their future form of the state of perfected correction.

Phase Two* finds them in the period of six thousand years, which are divided up into the two systems that we have already mentioned, the physical body and the Crude Spirit (*Nefesh*). They are then given the opportunity to work at the Torah and at the *Mitzvot* in order to transform the "will to receive" that they have in them into a "will to impart" pleasure to their Creator. For the duration of this Phase, no correction at all comes to the physical bodies but only to the Souls (*Nefesh*). That is to say, the Soul (*Nefesh*) has to destroy from itself every trace of the aspect of the "will to receive", which is an aspect of the physical body, and to remain purely in the aspect of the "will to impart", for this is the form of the will that is contained in the Soul (*Nefesh*). Even the Soul (*Nefesh*) of a completely righteous man will not be able to take delight in the Garden of Eden after death until all of the physical body has been decomposed in the earth.

---

* Time, space and motion have no place within the Endless World or what is known as Spirituality. These concepts relate only to the period after "restriction" or phase two.

The third Phase is the completion of the correction of the Souls after the resurrection of the dead, when the full correction will also reach the physical bodies. Then the actual receiving, which takes the form of the physical body, will be transformed and will take the form of pure imparting, and they will then become suited to receive all the goodness and delight and pleasantness that is in the Thought of Creation. Together with this they will achieve a very close attachment to their Creator because of their "similarity of form". They do not receive all this through their "will to receive", but rather through their "will to impart" pleasure to their Creator. By receiving from Him, they are in fact imparting as the Almighty gets pleasure when others receive from Him.

From now on, in order to be brief, I will be referring to these three Phases as Phase One, Phase Two and Phase Three. You should remember all that we have explained here about every one of the Phases.

Now, when you reflect on these three Phases, you will find that they each require the others, to the extent that were it possible for one of them to be eliminated, all of them would stop. For example, if Phase Three, which is the transformation of the receiving into the imparting, did not become manifest, then necessarily Phase One which is found in the "Endless" Blessed Be He, could never have become manifest. For the full perfection could only leave the "Endless" because that which was to take place in Phase Three was already there in His Eternity as part of the present. The perfection that is depicted in that Phase is merely a transference from the future to His present. However, if it were possible for that future to disappear, there would then be no existence in the present. Phase Three requires of necessity the existence of all that is in Phase One. This is even more true for a situation in which any part of Phase Two would disappear. For in this Phase there is to be found all the work that will eventually be completed in Phase Three, namely the work of "ruin", of "correction" and "repair", and of the continued elevation of the levels of the Souls. Without this, how could Phase Three possibly follow? Similarly, Phase Two requires Phase Three, and also the existence of Phase One in the Blessed "Endless". For the full perfection that will be found in Phase Three already exist there. This necessarily requires that Phases Two and Three will actually appear in full with that perfection which is already there, without any additions or without anything missing. So it is Phase One itself that of necessity requires the two systems to be spread out parallel to each other in Phase Two in order to allow the physical body with its "defective will to receive" to enter into the system of Uncleanness which will in turn make its "correction" possible. If there were no system of the worlds of Uncleanness, we would never possess this "will to receive", then it would not be possible for us to "correct" it and so reach Phase Three; for a man cannot correct what he does not possess. It is therefore impossible to ask how the whole system of Uncleanness could possibly be brought into being by Phase One, for on the contrary, it is in fact Phase One that requires its existence and then its continued preservation in Phase Two.

This does not really provide a basis for asking "If this is so, then in fact we have been deprived of any freedom of choice, heaven forbid, since according to this we are compelled to attain to Phase Three by force of its already being an integral part of Phase One?'' The explanation is that the Almighty prepared two paths for us in Phase Two that will lead us to Phase Three. The first is the path of the observance of the Torah and of the *Mitzvot*, as we explained previously. The second path is the path of agony and torment, in which it is the torments that scourge the physical body and compel us to finally transform the "will to receive" that we have in us to accept the form of the "will to impart" and become closely attached to the Almighty. This is in line with that which our Sages of blessed memory stated in the Talmud (*Sanhedrin*, 97b): "If you return to the right path it will be good, but if you do not I shall set over you a king like Haman, and he will restore you to the right path against your wills." This is also what they referred to in their comments on the verse in Isaiah "I will hasten it on, in its time." (*Isaiah*, 60:22) "If they are righteous I will hasten it on, but if not it will be in its time." The explanation of this is that if we are righteous by following the first path, that is through the observance of the Torah and the *Mitzvot*, then we hasten on our "correction" (*Tikun*) and we then have no need of any harsh or bitter torments, nor of a prolonged period of time that will be sufficient for us to receive these so that they might bring us back to the right path against our wishes. The punishments that Souls (*Neshamot*) receive in hell are part of the path of torments. However, whatever path one may follow, the final result of the "correction" (*Tikun*), which is in fact Phase Three, has already been necessitated and determined by Phase One. Thus the entire freedom of choice that we possess is confined to the ability to choose between the path of torments

and between the path of Torah and *Mitzvot*. We have thus
explained how these three Phases of the souls (*Neshamot*) are
connected with each other, and how each Phase necessitates
the existence of the others.

This explanation should assist in understanding the third
question that we posed at the beginning: self-reflection reveals
to us our imperfections and our lowly position. Yet how is
this possible, seeing that we have been created by the Holy
One whose perfect agency must necessarily produce perfect
works? However, according to what we have just explained,
it should now be perfectly understood that the body that we
possess, with all its insignificant components and categories,
is not really our true body; that is to say, the eternal one
that is completely perfect is to be found already existing in
the Blessed "Endless" in the aspect of Phase One. It is there
that it receives its perfect form from that which will ultimately
come about in Phase Three, namely "receiving in the form of
imparting", which is a state that is "similar in form" to the
Blessed "Endless". Therefore, it is Phase One that requires
that Phase Two contain the shell (*Kelipah*) of that body that
we possess in its despicable and imperfect form — namely the
"will to receive" for itself alone which is a force that brings
separation from the Blessed "Endless". It is given to us in
Phase Two so that we should "correct" it so that it should be
possible for us to receive our eternal body in Phase Three. We
should not have any complaints at all about that. Our work
cannot be conceived of as happening only in this perishable
body. We are constantly to be found, even in Phase Two,
in that degree of perfection that is fitting and appropriate
for the perfect Creator who created us. This body does not

blemish us in any way for it will perish and disappear. It has only been prepared for us for the amount of time that is necessary for us to eliminate it and so receive our eternal form.

This explanation should now also provide an answer for the fifth question that we originally posed: How is it possible that from the Eternal, who has no beginning or end, there should come forth finite, perishable beings? However, according to what has been explained here it should be understood that we did in fact go forth from him as eternal creatures with full perfection, as befits His Eternity. But this eternity of ours necessarily demands that the shell (*Kelipah*) of the body that we are given merely for the sake of work should be finite and perishable. For if the shell (*Kelipah*) of the body should remain eternal, then we should remain constantly separated, heaven forbid, from eternal life. We have already stated (on page 20) that this form of our body, which is the "will to receive" for itself alone, is not to be found at all in the Eternal Thought of Creation. There we exist in the forms that are ours in Phase Three. However, we are compelled to possess this form in Phase Two so that it will be possible for us to correct it, as we have explained.

There is absolutely no basis for asking in this connection about the condition of the other creatures of the world besides man, for man is the centre of the whole creation as we will explain (on page 56). All the other creatures of the world have no value or worth in themselves, but their worth is to be measured only according to the amount of assistance that they give a man in bringing him to perfection. Thus they ascend and descend with him, yet without any independent worth.

CHAPTER 6

SUFFER AND TORMENT

We shall now have an answer for the fourth question that we posed: Since it is in the nature of the good to do good, how did the Almighty create creatures that from the outset would be made to suffer and be tortured throughout their lives? As we have explained, all these torments are necessitated by our Phase One in which our complete eternity that is derived from Phase Three compels us to travel, either through the path of the Torah or through the path of torments (see on page 30). Yet all these torments only affect the shell (*Kelipah*) of this body of ours which was created solely for death and for being buried. This should teach us that the "will to receive for itself alone" was created only in order that it should be eradicated and removed from the world, so that it should be transformed into a "will to impart". All the torments that we suffer are merely manifestations that reveal the futility and the dangers that lie in wait for it.

Imagine for a moment that the entire population of the world was to unanimously agree to eliminate and destroy the "will to receive for themselves alone" that they have within them, then the only will a man should possess would be the "will to impart" to his fellow man. Then all worries and all harmful matters would disappear from the world, and everybody would be sure of a full and healthy life, for then every one of us would have a whole world of people that were worrying on his behalf and providing for his needs. However, at a time when everyone possesses only the "will to receive for himself alone", there appear all the worries, torments, wars and killings from which there is no escape, and which weaken our bodies with all kinds of pain and disease. Thus it is clear that all these torments that are to be found in our world are only manifestations that are set in front of us in order to propel us into eliminating the evil shell (*Kelipah*) of the body, and so into receiving the perfect form of the "will to impart". It is to this that we referred when we said that it is the path of torments that is capable of bringing us to the desired form. You should know that the *Mitzvot* that pertain between man and man have precedence over the *Mitzvot* that pertain between man and the Omnipresent, for imparting to one's fellow man brings one to imparting to the Omnipresent.

CHAPTER 7

OUR ESSENCE

We should have arrived now at the solution to the first question that we posed right at the beginning: What is the essence of our being? Our essence is the same as the essence of all that is in existence, which is no more nor less than the "will to receive". However, not as this essence occurs to us now in Phase Two, where it is the "will to receive for oneself alone", but rather as it exists in Phase One in the Blessed "Endless", that is to say in its eternal form which is "receiving in order to impart" pleasure to the Creator (page 27). Although we have not as yet actually reached Phase Three and we are still separated from it by time, this in no way harms our essence at all, for Phase Three is required and necessitated by Phase One, therefore "whatever will eventually be collected is as good as collected now". As for the time factor which is usually reckoned to be a drawback, this is only true in a case where there is some doubt as to whether that which has to be completed will be completed in the alloted time; however, since here there is absolutely no doubt at all, it is as if we had already reached Phase Three. Thus the body that we possess now in its evil form can in no way harm our essence, seeing that it and all that pertains to it will be eliminated together with the whole system of Uncleanness which is their source, and "whatever will eventually be burned is as good as burned now"; it will thus be considered as if it never existed. However the Crude Spirit (*Nefesh*) that is clothed by that body — the essence of which also consists only of the aspect of the "will" which is the "will to impart" which proceeds to us from the system of the four worlds of Emanation, Creation, Formation, and Making of Holiness (see page 24) — exists for all eternity, for this form of the "will to impart" has a "similarity of form" to the Giver of life, and is under no circumstances interchangeable, heaven forbid. (We will elaborate further on this theme on page 50).

Do not permit your heart to go astray after the views of the philosophers who maintain that the actual essence of the soul (*Nefesh*) is a rational substance, and that its existence comes only by virtue of the thoughts which it thinks and to which it owes its existence. They also claim that the continuation of the soul (*Nefesh*) after the death of the body depends entirely on the amount of rationality and intellectual understanding that it has received, to the extent that if it lacks intellectual understanding there is nothing at all on which the continued existence of the soul (*Nefesh*) can depend. This is by no means the view of the Torah, it is also not even acceptable to the rational mind. For every person that has attempted at one time to acquire intellectual understanding knows and feels that intellectual understanding is an acquisition that is acquired and is not the acquirer himself. But rather, as we have already explained, all the substance of the renewed creation, whether it be the substance of spiritual objects or the substance of physical objects, is no more nor less than the "will to receive". Although we stated that the soul (*Nefesh*) consists entirely of the "will to impart", this is merely by virtue of the corrections (*Tikun*) of the "clothing of returning light" that it receives from the higher worlds where it originally came to us — the whole subject of this clothing has been explained in the "Introduction to the Wisdom of the Kabbalah". (However, the very essence of the soul (*Nefesh*) consists also of the "will to receive", and an examination of the references that we have mentioned should help you to understand this).

Thus, the only way that a distinction can be made between one object and another is through the "will" that they contain, for it is the "will" in every essence that gives birth to its needs and it is the needs that give birth to the thoughts and concepts in appropriate amounts so that those needs that the "will to receive" has brought into being will be attained. In the same way that the "wills" of all men are different from each other, so are their needs and their thoughts different from each other. For example, those men in whom the "will to receive" is confined to only animal lusts, their needs and their thoughts and the learning that they have acquired exist only in order to gratify this "will" in all its animal fullness. Even though they make use of rational understanding of knowledge just as a human being, yet a slave is never more than its master, thus it is an animal understanding that is subjected to serve the animal "will".

As for those whose "will to receive" is directed in the main towards human lusts, such as honor and domination over others, lusts which are not to be found among animals, most of their needs, and consequently their thoughts and minds, are directed to gratifying that "will" as much as is possible.

For those people whose "will to receive" is directed in

the main towards rational matters, most of their needs, their thoughts and their minds are directed towards gratifying this "will" to its fullest.

These three types of "will" are to be found in all members of the human race, however, they are blended in each individual in different proportions, and it is this that makes for the differences that exist between one man and another. These physical qualities can also serve as an analogy for the qualities of the spiritual bodies according to their spiritual value; thus the spiritual souls (*Nefesh*) of mankind, which by virtue of the "clothings of returning light" which they receive from the sublime worlds from which they come, possess only the "will to impart" pleasure to their Creator, for this "will" is, as we have explained, the actual essence of the soul (*Nefesh*). And it is after that it has become clothed in the physical body of a man that it gives birth in it to needs and to thoughts which will enable it to gratify its "will to impart" fully, which is achieved by imparting pleasure to its Creator in proportion to the "will" that is within it.

Since the essence of the physical body consists only of the "will to receive for itself alone", and all that is part of this body and attached to it is imbued with this defective "will to receive" — which from the outset was only created so that it should be eliminated and eradicated from the world so that the perfect and complete Phase Three which is at the end of the "correction" (*Tikun*) should be reached — it and all that appertains to it is of necessity mortal and perishable, just like a passing shadow that leaves no trace behind it. Since the essence of the soul (*Nefesh*) consists only in the "will to impart" which was already existent in the eternal Phase One and will exist in Phase Three that is inevitably due, it is therefore not perishable nor interchangeable, but rather it and all that pertains to it are eternal, existing forever. Thus the absence of form at the time of death has no effect on them at all, on the contrary, the absence of the form of the defective physical body serves to strengthen it even more so that it is then able to ascend to the heights of the Garden of Eden. It should now be clear that the continuity of the soul (*Nefesh*) has absolutely no dependence at all on the amount of rational understanding that it has acquired, which is what the philosophers maintain, but its eternalness lies only in its essence, that is to say in the "will to impart". As for the thoughts that it has acquired, these are rewards that it has received not it itself.

CHAPTER 8

RESURRECTION OF THE DEAD

This explanation now provides us with a full answer to the fifth question that we posed: Since the physical body is so defective, to the extent that the soul (*Nefesh*) does not exist in a state of purity until the body has completely decomposed in the earth, why then does it rise again at the time of the Resurrection of the Dead? This will also assist us in understanding the saying of our Sages of blessed memory: "The dead will be resurrected in the future with all their infirmities so that they should not say "He is not the same!" (*Zohar*, *Emor* 91a).

You will be able to understand this matter fully from the Thought of Creation itself, that is to say from Phase One. For we stated that since the whole Thought of Creation was in order to give pleasure to the creatures that He created, then necessarily He obviously created a very extensive "will to receive" all that good abundance that is in the Thought of Creation. For great pleasure and the will to receive it go together (see page 17). We explained there that this immense "will to receive" is the only "new" substance that He actually created, because there was no need for more than that in order to bring into existence the Thought of the Creation. It is of the nature of the Perfect Craftsman that he does not make anything that is superfluous, as we find in the Hymn of Unity: "In all Your work You did not forget one thing, You did not omit anything nor did You make anything additional".

We also explained there that this extensive "will to receive" was removed completely from the system of Holiness and placed in the system of the worlds of Uncleanness, from which the bodies derive their existence and their sustenance and all that pertains to them in this world, until the time when a man reaches the age of thirteen years.* For it is then, through occupying himself with the Torah through Kabbalah, that he begins to attain the soul (*Nefesh*) of holiness, which is then sustained from the system of worlds of Holiness in proportion to the holiness that the soul (*Nefesh*) attains.

Previously we also explained that for the duration of the period of six thousand years which has been given us for labouring at the Torah via the Kabbalah and at the *Mitzvot*, the body, or in other words the extensive "will to receive" that is within it, receives absolutely no "correction" (*Tikun*) at all from these, but all the "correction" (*Tikun*) that is achieved through our work only reach the Soul (*Nefesh*) which then ascends to higher stages in holiness and purity. This means that study of the Torah through Kabbalah and the performance of the *Mitzvot* serve only to enlarge the "will to impart" that is extended with the Soul (*Nefesh*). It is for this reason that the body will finally die and be buried and then decompose, for it has never received any correction (*Tikun*)

---

* Till thirteen, light that is in all of us is dormant. After this age only can we begin to restrict our "desires" for ourselves alone, for the metaphysical, psychological ability to restrict vis-à-vis ones' intensive "desire to receive" for oneself has now become part and parcel of the individual.

for itself. However, it is impossible that it should remain in this state, for after all, if the extensive "will to receive" was to disappear from the world then the Thought of Creation could not exist, heaven forbid; by this I mean that all the great delights whereby He intended to give pleasure to His creatures would then not be received, for an immense "will to receive" and great pleasure go hand in hand. According to the proportion that the "will to receive" is diminished so also in that same proportion is the pleasure and enjoyment derived from receiving also diminished.

We stated previously that Phase One necessitates that Phase Three should proceed with the full proportions that are to be found in the Thought of Creation as it is in Phase One, and that nothing at all should be lacking from it (see page 30). Therefore, Phase One necessitates the resurrection of the dead bodies. That is to say the extensive "will to receive" which they possess, which has already perished and become decomposed in Phase Two, is forced to be brought to life all over again with all their infirmities without any restrictions at all. Work then commences right from the beginning in order to transform this extensive "will to receive" into "receiving in order to impart". And in the course of this, two things will have been gained:

1. That we should have a place to receive all the good, the pleasure and the tenderness that is in the Thought of Creation, by virtue of the fact that we already have a body that is saturated with the "will to receive" which, as we have already explained, necessarily comes together with these pleasures.

2. Since our receiving in such a manner will only be in amounts that will impart pleasure to our Creator, then this

receiving is considered as pure imparting (see page 24). There-fore we shall arrive at a "similarity of form", which is close attachment (*Deveikuth*) which is our form in Phase Three. Thus Phase One obviously necessitates the resurrection of the dead.

However, the resurrection of the dead can only occur in proximity to the completion of the "correction" (*Tikun*), that is to say at the end of Phase Two. For after we have managed to negate the extensive "will to receive" that we possess, and we have received this "will" only so as to be capable of im-parting, then by means of our work at negating this "will to receive", we have succeeded in attaining to all the mar-velous levels that are in the soul (*Nefesh*) — which are termed Crude Spirit (*Nefesh*), Spirit (*Ruah*), Soul (*Neshamah*), Living (*Hayyah*) and Individual (*Yehidah*). Then we shall have at-tained to the greatest possible perfection, to the extent that it will be possible for the body to be brought to life again together with its extensive "will to receive" and it will no longer be able to harm us by separating us from our close attachment to the Almighty. On the contrary, we shall take control of it, and we shall give it the form of imparting, as has been explained earlier. In fact, a similar method is appli-cable to any bad personal characteristic that one may happen to possess but of which one would like to be rid. We would first of all have to remove it completely so that absolutely nothing of it remains, then after having done this it will be possible to receive it back again and then direct it along a middle path. But as long as we have not yet removed it com-pletely from ourselves, it will be absolutely impossible to direct it along the desired middle way.

This is what was intended when our Sages of blessed memory stated that the dead will be resurrected in the future with all their infirmities, and only after that will they be healed. For as has been stated earlier, at the very outset there occurs a resurrection of the body — which is the extensive "will to receive" — without any limits or restrictions at all, that is to say just as it developed in the chariot of the worlds of Uncleanness before they succeeded in purifying it somewhat through Kabbalah and the *Mitzvot*, and this would then be with all its infirmities. After this, it will be possible to proceed to the new task of causing this extensive "will to receive" to be channeled into a form of imparting and then it will be healed, for then it will have also achieved a "similarity of form". Our Sages of blessed memory explained that the reason for this resurrection is in order that they should not say that he is another, the explanation of which is that they should not say that he is in a different form than he was in the Thought of Creation. For there, this extensive "will to receive" was ready to receive all the good that was in the Thought of Creation, but in the meantime it had been given over to the "shells" (*Kelipot*), and then afterwards given over for purification. In the final event it is impossible that it should be another body, for if its proportions should be diminished in any way it would then be like a completely different body, and then it would not be at all suitable to receive any of the good that is in the Thought of Creation as it was receiving there in Phase One. This should be well understood.

CHAPTER 9

CHAIN OF EXISTENCE

All that has now been explained should provide us with an answer to the second question that we posed at the beginning of this introduction which was: What is our function in the long chain of existence in which we are, during the short number of years of our lives, but small links? You should know that our work for the duration of the seventy years of our lives can be divided up into four periods.

1. The first period is the period during which one obtains the extensive "will to receive" without any limits or restrictions, in all its full defective proportions, from the system of the four unclean worlds of Emanation, Creation, Formation, and Making. If we did not have within us this defective "will to receive" we would then not be capable of "correcting" it, for one cannot correct what one does not possess. Therefore, the "will to receive" is implanted in the body at birth upon its' entering this world. In addition, it is necessary that there should be a chariot for the unclean "Shells" (*Kelipot*) for a period of not less than thirteen years, that is to say, the "Shells" should dominate him and give him of their lights, and it is these lights of the "Shells" (*Kelipot*) that expand his "will to receive". For the gratification that the "Shells" (*Kelipot*) provide for the "will to receive" serve only to expand the demands of the "will to receive". For

example, when a man is born he may only have a desire for one hundred of something and no more, but as soon as the Other Forces (of evil) grant him this hundred the "will to receive" immediately expands and he desires two hundred. Then after the Other Forces (of evil) have given him the two hundred in full, the "will to receive" immediately expands and he then desires four hundred. If he then does not manage to grow strong by means of the Kabbalah and of the *Mitzvot* so as to purify the "will to receive" and transform it into imparting, then his "will to receive" will expand continually, every year of his life until a man would then die having gratified not even half of his desires. A man undergoes this experience while he is in the domain of the Other Forces (of evil) whose function it is to expand and enlarge his "will to receive" and to make it extensive, without any limits at all. This is in order to provide a man with all the material he needs at which he may work and so effect a "correction" (*Tikun*).

2. The second period extends from the period when a man reaches thirteen years of age and upwards, for it is then that strength is given to a "point in his heart" where are to be found the five hindmost* parts of the Soul (*Nefesh*) that is clothed with its "will to receive" from the time of its birth. However, this does not begin to stir until after a man passes his thirteenth year, for then he begins to enter into the domain of the system of the worlds of Holiness in proportion to the amount* of his occupying himself with the Torah and with

---

* This amount metaphysically speaking, will depend to the degree of the individuals' transforming — vis-à-vis the conditioning system of Torah through Kabbalah and Precepts — his "desire to receive for oneself" to a "desire to impart". Obviously, no

the *Mitzvot*. But his main task will then be to achieve, and then enlarge and expand, his spiritual "will to receive" (on the basis of imparting).

From the time of his birth he possesses only the "will to receive" material things alone, therefore, even though he has achieved an extensive "will to receive" before he was thirteen years of age he will not yet have achieved the complete "will to receive", for it is only in spiritual matters that the "will to receive" will be extended and enlarged. For example, before a man reaches thirteen years of age his "will to receive" possesses a tremendous yearning to encompass all the wealth and glory in this material world, even though it is manifestly obvious to everybody that this world will not continue forever, but rather it exists for him like a shadow that passes by and then is gone and is no more. This is not the case when he achieves the extensive spiritual "will to receive", for then he wishes to encompass for his pleasure all the good and the riches that are in the everlasting world to come, which would then be for him an eternal acquisition that will last forever. Thus the principal "will to receive" only becomes complete with the "will to receive" spiritual objects.

It is this that is referred to in the *Tikkunim* (*Tikkunim Hadashim*, 97b) on the verse in Proverbs (30:15) "The horse-leech has two daughters crying 'Give! Give!'." It is explained then, that the horseleech represents Hell and that the wicked who are trapped in this Hell cry out like dogs "Give! Give!", that is to say, "Give us the wealth of this world, give us the wealth of the world to come." Yet despite all this, this

---

reference is made to the physical time as we know it on this mundane level.

level is incalculably superior to the first level, for besides the fact that he achieves through it the full extent of the "will to receive", then he is given all the material that he may need for this task, this is also a level that brings him to the level of "doing something for its own sake". As our Sages of blessed memory have said "Always let a man occupy himself with the Torah and with the *Mitzvot*, even not for their own sakes, for doing not for their own sakes leads to doing for their sakes." (*Pesahim*, 50b). Thus inevitably this level, which is reached after thirteen years, becomes refined into an aspect of holiness, and this is according to the 'secret' (*Sod*) of 'the handmaid of holiness who serves her mistress' which is the 'secret' (*Sod*) of the holy *Shechinah*. For the handmaid brings to doing for its own sake, and so he comes to merit the inspiration of the *Shechinah*. However, he needs to take all the appropriate steps that will bring him to doing "for its own sake", for if he does not make the effort and does not attain the level of doing "for its own sake", heaven forbid, then he will fall into the trap of the handmaid of Uncleanness, which is the counterpart of the handmaid of Holiness, whose function it is to confuse a man so that his doing "not for its own sake" will not bring him to doing "for its own sake". It is with reference to this that the Verse (Proverbs, 30:23) states: "and a handmaid that is heir to her mistress", for such a 'handmaid' will never allow a man to come near to her mistress, who is the holy *Shechinah*. The highest level of this period is reached when a man becomes in love with the Holy One, Blessed be He, with a very great passion, in a similar way to that of a man who falls in love with a physical lust to the extent that this lust never disappears from his mind right through the day and right through the night. A poet once described this state in the words: "When I remember Him He does not allow me to sleep". Of such a person it is then said that: "A desire fulfilled is a tree of life". (Proverbs, 13:12), for the 'secret' (*Sod*) of the 'Tree of life' is in the five levels of the Soul (*Neshamah*) whose period of duration lasts for five hundred years — every level lasting for one hundred years — which will be completed when a man receives all the five aspects of Crude Spirit (*Nefesh*), Spirit (*Ruah*), Soul (*Neshamah*), Living (*Hayyah*) and Individual (*Yehidah*); these will all be explained in the course of the third period.

The third period consists of working at the Torah and at the *Mitzvot* for "their own sakes", that is to say in order to "impart" and not in order to receive a reward. It is this work that purifies the "will to receive" that is within a man, and transforms it into "will to impart", which, in accordance with the proportion of the purity of his "will to receive", will then become fit and suitable to receive the five parts of the Soul (*Nefesh*) — termed Crude Spirit (*Nefesh*), Spirit (*Ruah*), Soul (*Neshamah*), Living (*Hayyah*) and Individual (*Yehidah*) — which are to be found in the "will to receive". However, these cannot become clothed by his body for as long as his "will to receive" dominates him; it is then to be found in a complete "opposite form" to the Soul (*Nefesh*), or at least in a "difference of form". The matter of 'clothing' and of "similarity of form" go hand in hand (as we explained previously on page 24). Thus at the time that a man achieves becoming fully immersed in the "will to impart" and not a trace remains of his own needs, then he has merited a "similarity of form" to his higher Crude Spirit (*Nefesh*), Spirit (*Ruah*), Soul (*Neshamah*), Living (*Hayyah*) and Individual (*Yehidah*) — which extend from their source in the Blessed "Endless" from Phase One by way of the Emanation, Creation, Formation, and Making of holiness. They extend to him immediately and become clothed in him in a gradual way.

The fourth period consists of the work that takes place after the resurrection of the dead. For then after the "will to receive" has been completely eliminated through death and burial, it comes to life again in a most extensive and vile "will to receive" which is in accordance with the 'secret' (*Sod*) of "The dead will be resurrected in the future with their infirmities" (see page 32), but they will then transform this into "receiving in the form of imparting", as I have already explained there at length. However, there are a few outstanding individuals to whom this task has been alloted now during their lifetimes in this world rather than awaiting the resurrection.

CHAPTER 10

THE NEED FOR SPIRITUAL WORLDS

We have yet to explain the sixth query that we posed in the beginning of this introduction: Our Sages of blessed memory stated that all the worlds, higher and lower, were only created for the sake of man. Yet at first sight it seems very surprising that all these were created for the sake of an insignificant man whose value is not even equal to that of a single hair when compared with the whole of existence that exists before us in this world, and this is even more true when he is compared with higher spiritual worlds; why then should the Almighty take the trouble to create all of these for his sake? And even more surprising: What need has a man for all these numerous and mighty spiritual worlds? However, you should know that the pleasure that Our Creator receives in imparting to His creatures depends entirely on the amount that these creatures feel that He is the Imparter, and that He it is who is giving them pleasure, for then He becomes very delighted with them, just like a father who is delighted with his loved son. It is to the extent that a son feels and recognizes the greatness and high position of his father, that his father will then show him the treasures that he has prepared for him. As the verse states (*Jeremiah*, 31:19): "Is Ephraim a darling son unto Me? Is he a child of delights? For as often as I speak of him, I do earnestly remember him still; therefore My bowels yearn for

him, I will surely have compassion on him, says the Lord.''
When you examine this verse closely you will be able to perceive and understand that the greatest delights of the Almighty
are with those perfect ones who have merited being aware of
Him, and recognizing His greatness in all those ways that He
has prepared for them, to the extent that He has a relationship with them similar to that of a father to his darling son,
and as a father with his child of delight. However, we shall
not delve into this subject at length, for it is sufficient for us
to know that it was for the sake of His pleasure and delight
with these perfect ones that it was worth His while to create
all the worlds, the upper and lower worlds, as will be explained later.

CHAPTER 11

THE FOUR LEVELS

The Holy One, Blessed be He, decided to prepare His creatures to reach the high and lofty level that we have mentioned by means of an ordered system of four levels that develop out of each other; these are termed Inanimate, Vegetative, Animal and Human. These are in reality the four aspects of the "will to receive" into which every single world of the upper worlds is divided. Although the ultimate purpose is in the fourth aspect of the "will to receive", it is impossible that the fourth aspect should become manifest all at once, but only by force of the other three aspects that preceed it. For it becomes manifest and develops in them and through them slowly and gradually until it attains its full perfection in the fourth aspect (this has been explained in my book 'The Ten Luminous Emanations').

The first aspect of the "will to receive", which is termed Inanimate and which is the beginning of the manifestation of the "will to receive" in the material world, is merely a moving force that encompasses the whole of the Inanimate species, yet in its individual component parts no movement at all is visible to the eye. For the "will to receive" gives birth to needs and the needs give birth to movements that will be sufficient to achieve what is needed. Yet since the "will to receive" is only contained in it in a small measure it rules only over the whole species at one and the same time, and thus its rule over the individual components is not apparent.

The next level is the Vegetative aspect, which is the second aspect of the "will to receive" and the proportions that it contains are greater than the proportion in the Inanimate; thus the "will to receive" dominates every single one of its individual components. For every individual component part possesses its own individual movement which is diffused through its entire length and breadth and moves in the direction of the rising of the sun. Eating, drinking, and the excretion of waste are clearly seen amongst them to be the properties of every single component part. Yet despite this any individual or independent sensibility is not to be found amongst any of them.

On an even higher level than this, there is the species of Animal, which is the third aspect of the "will to receive". Its qualities are to a large extent already determined. This "will to receive" has already given birth to feelings in every individual component that are independent and individual, which is the particular life that every individual part possesses in a way that is different from others. However, the sensibility for others is not to be found among them, that is to say they do not have any capability at all of feeling sorry at the grief of another, or even of rejoicing at the joy of another.

Superior to all of them is the species of man for he is the fourth aspect of the "will to receive" which is now present in its final and full measure. The "will to receive" that is contained in him also works in him as does the feeling for others. If you should wish to know precisely how great is the difference between the third aspect of the "will to receive" that is to be found in the species of Animal and the fourth aspect of the "will to receive" that is to be found in the species of man, I will tell you that this is similar to one single creature being weighed in value against the entire existence. For the "will to receive" that is contained in the species of Animal, which is devoid of any feeling for others, can give birth to wants and needs only in proportion to that which that creature has implanted within it. Whereas man possesses within him feeling for others, and thus is able to feel that he is deficient of everything that another possesses. Therefore he becomes consumed with envy to acquire all that is to be found in the possession of the other. If he should possess a hundred of something, he will desire two hundred. Thus his wants and his needs are constantly multiplying until he wishes to swallow up everything that exists in the whole world.

We have explained that the whole purpose that is desired by the Almighty from the entire creation that He created is to give pleasure to His creatures, in order that they should recognize and acknowledge His Truth and His greatness. In this way they should receive from Him all the goodness and delight He has prepared for them in accordance with what has been explained in the verse "Is Ephraim a darling son unto Me? Is he a child of delights? etc.". You will find most clearly that this purpose cannot be applicable in the case of the Inanimate — namely the great spheres such as the earth, the moon and the sun, no matter their brilliant radiance and their size — nor does it apply to the Vegetative species, nor to the Animal species, for they do not possess any feeling for others, or even for those of their own kind that are similar to them. How then should the divine feelings and God's bestowing of good come to rest on them? Thus only mankind is able to receive this good since they are already prepared for it through feelings that they have for others who are of their own kind and similar to them. After they have laboured at the Torah through Kabbalah and at the *Mitzvot* which transform their "will to receive" into the "will to impart" and thus cause them to attain a "similarity of form" with their Creator, they receive all the levels that have been prepared for them in the higher worlds that are termed Crude Spirit (*Nefesh*), Spirit (*Ruah*), Soul (*Neshamah*), Living (*Hayyah*) and Individual (*Yehidah*). Through this work they shall become fit to receive the purpose of the Thought of Creation. Thus we see that the entire purpose of the intention of the Creation was none other than for the sake of man.

I know that this conclusion is not at all acceptable to quite a few philosophers who are unable to accept that man, who is base and worthless in their view, should be the centre of the entire, great and sublime creation. However, these philosophers are to be compared to a worm that was born inside a radish; it sits there and supposes that the whole world of the Holy One, Blessed be He is as bitter and as dark and as small as the radish in which it was born. However, when it manages to pierce the shell of the radish it becomes amazed and says "I thought the whole world was just like the radish in which I was born, but now I see in front of me a tremendous light and beautiful world!" Very similar are those who are totally immersed in the "shell" of their "will to receive" in which they were born, and they have never attempted to receive those special spices (the conditioning agents) — the Torah and the practical *Mitzvot* — which are capable of piercing through even this hard "shell" and of transforming it into a "will to impart pleasure to one's Creator". They are therefore compelled to maintain that man is insignificant and worthless, which is in effect their own condition. They are incapable of imagining that all this immense existence was created only for their sakes. However, if they should occupy themselves with Torah and with the *Mitzvot* so as to impart pleasure to their Creator in proper purity, they would come to pierce the "shell" of the "will to receive" in which they were born and so receive the "will to impart". Their eyes would then be immediately opened to see and to attain all the levels of wisdom, understanding and clear knowledge, that are so desirable and pleasant, which have been prepared for them in the spiritual worlds. Then they themselves would say what our Sages of blessed memory have said: "As for a good guest, what does he say? All the trouble the host has taken, he has taken only for my sake."*

---

* Talmud Berachot, p. 58a

CHAPTER 12

THE FIVE WORLDS

However, the question still remains: For what reason should a man have all these sublime worlds that the Almighty has created for his sake, and what need does a man have of them? You must know that all the worlds can generally be divided into five; these are termed: (i) *Adam Kadmon* - Primordial man. (ii) *Atziluth* - Emanation. (iii) *Beriah* - Creation. (iv) *Yetzirah* - Formation. (v) *Asiyah* - Making. Each one of these has innumerable components. These five worlds are aspects of the five *Sefirot* — *Keter* (crown), *Hokhmah* (wisdom), *Binah* (intelligence), *Tiferet* (beauty) and *Malkhut* (kingdom). The world of *Adam Kadmon* (Primordial man) is *Keter* (crown), the world of Emanation is *Hokhmah* (wisdom), the world of Creation is *Binah* (intelligence), the world of Formation is *Tiferet* (beauty), and the world of Making is *Malkhut* (kingdom). The lights that are clothed in these five worlds are termed *Yehidah* (Individual), *Hayyah* (Living), *Neshamah* (Soul), *Ruah* (Spirit) and *Nefesh* (Crude Spirit). For the light of the *Yehidah* (Individual) radiates in the world of Primordial man (*Adam Kadmon*). The light of *Hayyah* (Living) radiates in the world of Emanation. The light of *Neshamah* (Soul) radiates in the world of Creation. The light of *Ruah* (Spirit) radiates in the world of Formation, and the light of *Nefesh* (Crude Spirit) in the world of Making. All these worlds, and all that is within them, are included in the Holy Name *Yod Hei Vav Hei** and the upper tip of the *Yod*. Man is incapable of knowing the first world, which is that of Primordial man (*Adam Kadmon*), therefore, it is alluded to only in the upper tip of the *Yod* of the Holy Name, and we do not talk of it. Thus, we make constant mention of only the four worlds of Emanation, Creation, Formation, and Making. The *Yod* is the world of Emanation (*Atzilut*) and the *Hei* is the world of Creation (*Beriah*) the *Vav* the world of Formation (*Yetzirah*), and the lower *Hei* is the world of Making (*Asiyah*).

We have now explained the five worlds which contain the entire spiritual existence that extends from the Blessed "Endless" to this present world. However, they all contain each other. In fact, as has been mentioned previously, every single world contains all the five worlds, namely the five *Sefirot*, *Keter* (crown), *Hokhmah* (wisdom), *Binah* (intelligence), *Tiferet* (beauty) and *Malkhuth* (kingdom), clothe within them the five lights of Crude Spirit (*Nefesh*), Spirit (*Ruah*), Soul (*Neshamah*), Living (*Hayyah*) and Individual (*Yehidah*) which correspond to the five worlds. Apart from these five *Sefirot* that are to be found in every single one of these five worlds, there are also the four spiritual aspects — Inanimate, Vegetative, Animal and Human. The Soul (*Neshamah*) of a man is the Human aspect, the Angels constitute the Animal aspect, the Vegetative aspects are termed garments, and the Inanimate aspects are termed halls, and they are distinguished as clothing one another. For the aspects of Human, namely the Souls (*Neshamot*) of mankind, are clothed around the five divine

---

* These are the Hebrew letters of the Holy Name that spell out the Tetragrammaton.

Sefirot Keter (crown), *Hokhmah* (wisdom), *Binah* (intelligence), *Tiferet* (beauty) and *Malkhut* (kingdom) which constitute the divineness in each world. (The fact of the divinity of the ten *Sefirot* will be explained further on in my Introduction to the Book of the Zohar). The Animal aspects, namely the Angels, clothe the Souls (*Neshamot*), and the Vegetative aspects, which are the garments, clothe the Angels. The Inanimate aspects, namely the halls, are wrapped around all of these. This being wrapped around one another is assumed, inasmuch as all make use of one another and develop from each other, as we demonstrated in our explanation of the physical Inanimate, Vegetative, Animal and Human aspects that are in this world (see pages 52-56). We also explained there that the three aspects of Inanimate, Vegetative and Animal do not have any existence for themselves, but only exist so that the fourth aspect, which is the species of man, should develop and become elevated by means of them; thus their sole function is to serve man and be useful to him. The same is true for all the spiritual worlds in which the three aspects, Inanimate, Vegetative and Animal are to be found; they only exist to serve and be of use to the Human aspect which is the Soul (*Neshamah*) of a man. Therefore, all these are clothed over the Soul (*Neshamah*) of a man, which means that they exist for his benefit.

As soon as a man is born, he possesses an aspect of the Soul (*Nefesh*) of holiness. Not the actual Soul itself but rather the hindmost aspect of the Soul (*Nefesh*), which is the last of its aspects, termed because of its minuteness — a point. This point is clothed in a man's heart, that is to say, in the "will to receive" that is within him which manifests itself principally in a man's heart. You must know this general rule, which is that everything that appertains to the whole of existence in its entirety, appertains to every single world, even to the minutest part which it is possible to specify. Thus it follows that just as the five *Sefirot Keter* (crown), *Hokhmah* (wisdom), *Binah* (intelligence), *Tiferet* (beauty) and *Malkhut* (kingdom) are present in the whole of existence, these five *Sefirot* are also present in every single world. These five *Sefirot* are also present in every single small part that is in that world. We have already stated that this present world is divided up into the four aspects Inanimate, Vegetative, Animal and Human which correspond to the four *Sefirot*: *Hokhmah* (wisdom), *Binah* (intelligence), *Tiferet* (beauty), and *Malkhut* (kingdom). For the Inanimate corresponds to *Malkhut* (kingdom), the Vegetative corresponds to *Tiferet* (beauty), the Animal corresponds to *Binah* (intelligence), the Human corresponds to *Hokhmah* (wisdom), and the root of all of them corresponds to *Keter* (crown). However, as has been stated every single member of all the species that are included in the categories of Inanimate, Vegetative, Animal and Human also has present in it the four aspects of Inanimate, Vegetative, Animal and Human in such a way that even in a single member of the Human species, that is to say even in an individual human being, there are also to be found in him the four aspects of Inanimate, Vegetative, Animal and Human which are four parts of the "will to receive" that is in him, and in which the point of the Soul (*Nefesh*) of holiness is clothed.

CHAPTER 13

SPIRITUAL ESSENCE AND ELEVATION

Prior to a man's reaching thirteen years of age, the point that is in his heart is not at all manifest. But after he has reached the age of thirteen when he begins to occupy himself with the Torah and the *Mitzvot*, even though this may be without the appropriate concentration, — that is to say, without being full of love and fear as befits one serving the King — and it may be "not for its own sake", yet the point that is in his heart begins to grow and to make itself felt. For the performance of the *Mitzvot* does not require specific concentration, thus even actions that are performed without specific concentration are capable of purifying a man's "will to receive", but only up to the first level that is within him that is called Inanimate. It is in proportion to the amount that he purifies the Inanimate part of the "will to receive" that he will proceed to construct the 613 limbs of the point within his heart, which is the Inanimate part of the Soul (*Nefesh*) of holiness. Then when he has become complete through the performance of all the 613 *Mitzvot*, the 613 limbs of the point that is in the heart will also become complete. The 248 spiritual limbs are constructed by means of the observance of the 248 positive *Mitzvot*, and the 365 spiritual sinews are constructed by means of the observance of the 365 negative *Mitzvot*. Thus he will proceed until a complete *Parzuf* (countenance) of the Soul (*Nefesh*) of holiness is constituted, for then the Soul (*Nefesh*) will ascend and clothe* itself around the *Sefirah* of *Malkhut* (kingdom) which is in the spiritual world of Making. Then all the categories of the spiritual Inanimate, Vegetative, and Human parts that are in that world and which correspond to the *Sefirah* of *Malkhut* (kingdom) of the world of Making, will aid and assist the *Parzuf* (countenance) of the Soul (*Nefesh*) of the man that has ascended there; that is to say, to the extent that the Soul (*Nefesh*) has given them intellectual understanding. It is those concepts which become its spiritual food and which give it strength to multiply and become bigger so that it can extend the light of the *Sefirah* of *Malkhut* (kingdom) of the world of Making in all its desirable fullness, and so illuminate the man's physical body. For that perfect light helps a man to increase his efforts in Torah and *Mitzvot* and to receive the remaining levels. Just as we stated previously, as soon as the physical body of a man is born, a point from the light of the Soul (*Nefesh*) is born and becomes clothed within him, in this case as well, when his *Parzuf* (countenance) of the Soul (*Nefesh*) of holiness comes

---

* Light cannot illumine unless it has become enclothed in a "fitting vessel". A vessel, meaning the "desire to receive", by its very nature, is at opposite polarities to the "Light" whose basic characteristic is positive or imparting. Subsequently, for "Light" to become enclothed within a vessel, this severance which signifies the opposite polarity of the vessel or "desire to receive" for oneself must be removed and transformed into a vessel or "desire to receive" for the sake of imparting. In so being transformed, the vessel has created a "simularity of form" to the "Light". Consequently, as one moves up the ladder to phases of greater intensification of the "desire to receive" and transforms these vessels, then the ability to receive a superior quality of Light is increased, because the greater the vessel (metaphysically speaking the "desire to receive") the greater the content of Light.

into being, there comes into being with it a point from a level that is higher than it, which is the furthermost aspect of the light of the Spirit (*Ruah*) in the world of Making. This point clothes itself inside the innermost parts of the *Parzuf* countenance) of the Soul (*Nefesh*); the same process occurs in all the levels. Whenever a level comes into being, the furthermost aspect from the level that is above it extends into it. This connection between higher and lower extends to the highest levels, and it is this point that it possesses from the higher level that makes it capable of rising to that higher level. However, this is not the place to broach this subject at length.

The light of this Soul (*Nefesh*) is termed the Inanimate light of holiness of the world of Making. This is because it corresponds to the purity of the Inanimate part of the "will to receive" that is within a man's body. In addition, its light-giving actions in the spiritual realm are similar to the aspects of the Inanimate species in the material realm, which has been explained previously on page 54. That is to say, none of its components have any individual movement. Similarly the light of the *Parzuf* (countenance) of the Soul (*Nefesh*) of Making, even though it has 613 limbs which are 613 different forms for receiving the abundant light, these differences are not noticeable in it. All that is apparent is the total light which encompasses all equally without the individual parts being distinguishable.

You should know that even though the *Sefirot* are divine, and there is no change or difference in them from the top of the *Keter* (crown) which is in the world of primordial man (*Adam Kadmon*) to the end of the *Sefirah* of *Malkhut* (kingdom) which is in the world of Making, there is however, a great difference for those who receive them. For the *Sefirot* are referred to as lights and vessels. The light which is in the *Sefirot* is pure divinity, but the vessels which are called *Keter* (crown), *Hokhmah* (wisdom), *Binah* (intelligence), *Tiferet* (beauty) and *Malkhut* (kingdom) which are to be found in all of the three lower worlds that are called the worlds of Creation, Formation and Making are not themselves the aspect of divinity, but rather they are the aspects of covers that conceal the light of the Blessed "Endless" that is in them. They measure out a fixed amount of lumination to those who receive so that each one should only receive in accordance with the proportion of purity that is in him. From this aspect, even though the light itself is only one, we term the lights in the *Sefirot* — Crude Spirit (*Nefesh*), Spirit (*Ruah*), Soul (*Neshamah*), Living (*Hayyah*) and Individual (*Yehidah*). The light is divided up according to the nature of the vessels. The *Sefirah Malkhut* (kingdom) is the thickest cover that conceals the light of the Blessed "Endless". The light that it transmits from Him to those that receive it comes only in small amounts and is connected to the purity of only the Inanimate part of a man's body, consequently it is called *Nefesh* (Crude Spirit). Whereas the vessel of *Tiferet* (beauty) is more refined than the vessel of *Malkhut* (kingdom), and the light that it transmits from the Blessed "Endless" is connected to the purity of the Vegetative part of a man's body for it activates him more than the light of the *Nefesh* (Crude Spirit); it is termed the light of the *Ruah* (Spirit). The vessel of *Binah* (intelligence) is more refined than the vessel of *Tiferet* (beauty), and the light that it transmits from the Blessed "Endless" is connected to the purity of the Animal part that is in a man's body; this is termed the light of the *Neshamah* (Soul). However, the vessel of *Hokhmah* (wisdom) is more refined than all the others, and the light that it transmits from the Blessed "Endless" is connected to the purity of the Human part that is in a man's body; this is called the light of *Hayyah* (Living) and its effects are unlimited, as we will shortly explain.

As has been previously stated, there becomes clothed in the *Partzuf* (countenance) of the Soul (*Nefesh*) that a person acquires by means of occupying himself with Torah and the *Mitzvot* without the proper intention, a point from the light of the Spirit (*Ruah*). When a person fortifies himself to occupy himself with Torah and the *Mitzvot* with the correct intention, he gradually purifies the Vegetative part from the aspect of the "will to receive" that is in it, and he proportionately proceeds to construct the point of the Spirit (*Ruah*) to a whole *Partzuf* (countenance); for it is by means of the 248 positive *Mitzvot* that are performed with the proper intention that the point becomes diffused into its 248 spiritual limbs. Through the performance of the 365 negative *Mitzvot* the point becomes diffused into its 365 sinews. Then when it has been completely diffused throughout all of the 613 limbs it ascends and clothes the *Sefirah* of *Tiferet* (beauty) that is in the spiritual world of Making, which conveys to it from the Blessed "Endless" a superior light, termed the light of the Spirit (*Ruah*), which is directed to the purification of the Vegetative part of a man's body. Then all that pertains to the Inanimate, Vegetative and Animal parts that are in the world of Making which are related to the structure of *Tiferet* (beauty) aid the *Partzuf* (countenance) of the Spirit (*Ruah*) of man to receive the lights from the *Sefirah* of *Tiferet* (beauty) in all their fullness, in the same way that has been explained previously, (page 50) with regard to the light of the Crude Spirit (*Nefesh*). For this reason it is termed the Vegetative of holiness, thus the nature of its radiance resembles physical Vegetative matter, which, as we explained previously, already possesses many variations of movement that are recognizable in every single part of it. Similarly the light of the spiritual Vegetative part is so strong as to illuminate, in special ways, every single limb of the 613 limbs inclusive of 365 sinews that are in the *Partzuf* (countenance) of the Spirit (*Ruah*), and each one of them displays the power of action that is attributed to that limb. Furthermore, with the going out of the *Partzuf* (countenance) of the Spirit (*Ruah*), there also goes out with it the point of its highest level, that is to say the point of the light of the Soul (*Neshamah*) which is enclothed in innermost parts of the *Partzuf* (countenance).

It is by means of occupying himself with the esoteric secrets of the Torah and with the underlying reasons for the *Mitzvot* that a man purifies the Animal part from the "will to receive" that is in him, He then proportionately proceeds to construct the point of the Soul (*Neshamah*) that is clothed within him in its 248 limbs and 365 sinews. When the whole construction has been completed and the *Partzuf* (countenance) has been formed, it ascends and clothes the *Sefirah* of *Binah* (intelligence) which is in the spiritual world of Making; for this vessel is inestimably purer than the first vessel of *Tiferet* (beauty) and *Malkhut* (kingdom), and it transmits to him from the Blessed "Endless" a great light which is called the light of the *Neshamah* (Soul). All the parts of the Inanimate,

Vegetative and Animal that are in the world of Making, and which are related to the structure of *Binah* (intelligence), aid and assist the *Partzuf* (countenance) of the *Neshamah* (Soul) of a man to receive His lights in their entirety from the *Sefirah* of *Binah* (intelligence), in a similar way to that which has been explained in the case of the light of the Crude Spirit (*Nefesh*). This is also termed the Animal aspect of holiness, because it is directed to the purification of the Animal part that is in a man's body. Similarly, the nature of its illumination — as has been explained previously in the case of the physical Animal species (see page 50) — is that it gives a particular sensibility to each of the 613 limbs of the *Partzuf* (countenance) so that each of them is able to become alive and feel with an independent feeling without any dependence at all on the *Partzuf* (countenance) until it has been refined. For the 613 limbs that are in it are 613 *Partzufim* (countenances) which are all characterized by their particular ways of illumination, each one having its own particular way. The superiority of this light over the light of the spirit (*Ruah*) in the spiritual realm is equivalent to the difference in the physical realm between the Animal species on the one hand and the Inanimate and the Vegetative on the other hand. In this case also, a point goes out from the light of the *Hayyah* (Living) of holiness — which is the light of the *Sefirah* of *Hochmah* (wisdom) — together with the going out of the *Partzuf* (countenance) of the Soul (*Neshamah*) and it becomes enclothed in the innermost parts of the *Partzuf* (countenance).

After a man has attained that great light that is termed the light of the Soul (*Neshamah*) — which each of the 613 limbs of that *Partzuf* (countenance) illuminate with a full and radiant light that is reserved for each of them just like a *Partzuf* (countenance) that is reserved for itself — then the door is opened for him to occupy himself with each *Mitzvah* according to its true inner concentration; for every limb of the *Partzuf* (countenance) of the Soul (*Neshamah*) illuminates for him the paths of all the *Mitzvot* that are related to that limb. Thus with the great power of those lights he proceeds to purify all the Human part of his "will to receive" and to transform it into a "will to bestow". In this proportion, the point of the light of the *Hayyah* (Living) that is clothed within him is gradually built up in its 248 spiritual limbs and 365 spiritual sinews, then when a complete *Partzuf* (countenance) has been completed, it proceeds to ascend and clothe the *Sefirah* of *Hochmah* (wisdom) which is in the spiritual world of Making. The purity of this vessel is limitless, thus it transmits to him from the Blessed "Endless" a very great and powerful light, which is termed the light of the *Hayyah* (Living) or Soul (*Neshamah*) to Soul (*Neshamah*). Then all the parts of the world of Making, consisting of the Inanimate, Vegetative and Animal aspects which are related to the *Sefirah* of *Hochmah* (wisdom), assist him in receiving the light of the *Sefirah* of *Hochmah* (wisdom) in its entirety and perfection, in the same way that has been explained in the case of the light of the Crude Spirit (*Nefesh*). It is thus termed the Human of holiness because of its being directed to the purification of the Human part of a man's body. Similarly, the value of that light in godliness is equivalent to the value of the Human aspect in the Inanimate, Vegetative, Animal and Human of the physical realm, that is to say, it acquires feelings for others besides itself. The amount that this light is greater than the lights of the Inanimate, Vegetative, and Animal of the spiritual realm is also proportionate to the relative greatness of the Human aspect of the physical realm over the Inanimate, Vegetative and Animal aspects of the physical realm. The aspect of the light of the Blessed "Endless" that is clothed in this *Partzuf* (countenance) is termed the light of the *Yehidah* (Individual).

However, you should know that all of these five aspects of the lights — Crude Spirit (*Nefesh*), Spirit (*Ruah*), Soul (*Neshamah*), Living (*Hayyah*) and Individual (*Yehidah*) — that are received from the world of Making, are merely aspects of the Crude Spirit (*Nefesh*), Spirit (*Ruah*), Soul (*Neshamah*), Living (*Hayyah*) and Individual (*Yehidah*) of the light of the Crude Spirit (*Nefesh*). They therefore contain none of the aspect of the light of the Spirit (*Ruah*) at all. The light of the Spirit (*Ruah*) is only to be found in the world of Formation, and the light of the Soul (*Neshamah*) is only to be found in the world of Creation, and the light of the *Hayyah* (Living) is only to be found in the world of Emanation, and the light of the *Yehidah* (Individual) is only to be found in the world of Primordial man (*Adam Kadmon*). However, as we stated previously, whatever exists in the whole exists also in all the Individual parts, even in the most minute part. Thus all of the five aspects of Crude Spirit (*Nefesh*), Spirit (*Ruah*), Soul (*Neshamah*), Living (*Hayyah*) and Individual (*Yehidah*) are all also to be found in the world of Making; however, these will only be the Crude Spirit (*Nefesh*), Spirit (*Ruah*), Soul (*Neshamah*), Living (*Hayyah*) and Individual (*Yehidah*) of the Crude Spirit (*Nefesh*). In exactly the same way, all these five aspects of Crude Spirit (*Nefesh*), Spirit (*Ruah*), Soul (*Neshamah*), Living (*Hayyah*) and Individual (*Yehidah*) are to be found in the world of Formation, but these are only the five parts of the Spirit (*Ruah*). Similarly, all the five aspects are to be found in the world of Creation, and they are the five parts of the Soul (*Neshamah*). The same is true for the world of Emanation where they are the five parts of the light of the *Hayyah* (Living), and similarly for the world of Primordial Man (*Adam Kadmon*), where they are the five parts of the light of the *Yehidah* (Individual). The distinction between each one of the worlds and the others is to be understood along the lines of what we explained in distinguishing between each of the five aspects of the Crude Spirit (*Nefesh*), Spirit (*Ruah*), Soul (*Neshamah*), Living (*Hayyah*) and Individual (*Yehidah*) of Making.

CHAPTER 14

THE EFFECTS OF REPENTANCE

You should know that repentance and purity are not acceptable unless there is an absolute determination that there will be no returning to one's previous folly. This is the meaning of the passage "How long is repentance necessary? Until the Knower of all mysteries testifies that the sinner will never again return to his folly". We said that if a man should purify the Inanimate part of the "will to receive" that is within him, he will attain a *Partzuf* (countenance) of the Crude Spirit (*Nefesh*) of Making and will then proceed to ascend and clothe the *Sefirah* of *Malkhut* (kingdom) of Making. However this will only be the case if he irrevocably purifies the Inanimate part in such a way that he will never return to his previous state of folly. Only then may he ascend to the spiritual world of Making, for he will most surely possess a "similarity of form" to that world. As for the other levels that we mentioned, namely the Spirit (*Ruah*), Soul (*Neshamah*), Living (*Hayyah*) and Individual (*Yehidah*) of the world of Making — for which a purification of the corresponding Vegetative, Animal and Human parts of a man's "will to receive" must take place in order that they may clothe and receive their lights — in these cases the purity need not be absolutely permanent to the extent that the Knower of all mysteries should have to testify that the sinner will no longer regress to his former folly. The reason for this is that the whole world of Making with all of the five *Sefirot* — *Keter* (crown), *Hokhmah* (wisdom), *Binah* (intelligence), *Tiferet* (beauty) and *Malkhut* (kingdom) — which are in it are merely five parts of the aspect of *Malkhut* (kingdom) which is related to the purity of the Inanimate part alone; thus these five *Sefirot* are merely five parts of the *Sefirah* of *Malkhut* (kingdom). Once a man has succeeded in purifying at least part of the Inanimate part of the "will to receive" he will have attained to a "similarity of form" to the whole world of Making, for every *Sefirah* of the world of Making receives from the aspects that correspond to it in the worlds that are higher than it. For example, The *Sefirah Tiferet* (beauty) of Making receives from the world of Formation, which is totally the aspect of *Tiferet* (beauty) and the light of the Spirit (*Ruah*). The *Sefirah Binah* (intelligence) of Making receives from the world of Creation, which is entirely the aspect of Soul (*Neshamah*). The *Sefirah Hokhmah* (wisdom) of Making receives from the world of Emanation, which is entirely *Hokhmah* (wisdom) and the light of the Living (*Hayyah*). Although a man has only purified the Inanimate part permanently, however, if he should purify the other three parts of his "will to receive" even though he does not succeed in permanently purifying them, he will also be able to receive the Spirit (*Ruah*), Soul (*Neshamah*) and Living (*Hayyah*) from the *Tiferet* (beauty), *Binah* (intelligence) and *Hokhmah* (wisdom) of Making, but only temporarily. Whenever one of these three parts of his "will to receive" should become stirred, he will immediately lose these lights.

However, after he has succeeded in purifying the Vegetative

part of his "will to receive" permanently as well, he will ascend to the world of Formation permanently and he will there attain to the level of the Spirit (*Ruah*) permanently. He will then be able to receive the lights of the Soul (*Neshamah*) and of the Living (*Hayyah*) from the *Sefirot Binah* (intelligence) and *Hokhmah* (wisdom) that are there — which are refined into the Soul (*Neshamah*) of the Spirit (*Ruah*) and the Living (*Hayyah*) of the Spirit (*Ruah*) — even if he has not as yet succeeded in purifying absolutely and permanently the Animal and Human parts. After he has attained the permanent purification of the Vegetative part of his "will to receive" he will already have attained to a "similarity of form" to the entire world of Formation to the highest level; this is similar to that which has been explained in the case of the world of Making.

Thus after he has also purified the Animal part from the "will to receive" and transformed it into the "will to impart", until He who knows all mysteries can testify concerning him that he will never again return to his folly, he will then have attained to a "similarity of form" to the world of Creation, where he will ascend and receive even the light of the Soul (*Neshamah*) permanently. He may also ascend, by means of his purification of the Human part of his body, to the *Sefirah Hokhmah* (wisdom) and receive also the light of the Living (*Hayyah*) that is there, even though he may not have purified it permanently, as in the case in the worlds of Formation and Making. However, the light that radiates on him will also not be permanent.

When he will have succeeded in permanently purifying the Human part from his "will to receive", he will then have attained to a "similarity of form" to the world of Emanation and he will then ascend and receive there the light of the Living (*Hayyah*) permanently. Then when he attains yet more, he will attain to the light of the "Endless" and to the light of the Individual (*Yehidah*) that is clothed in the light of the Living (*Hayyah*); however, we will deal with this subject more fully elsewhere.

You should now have a clear understanding of the question that we posed previously (page 41): what reason is there for a man having all these sublime worlds that the Almighty created for him, and what need does he have of them? For you should now be able to understand that it is absolutely impossible for a man to be able to give pleasure to his Creator without the assistance of all these worlds. For it is in proportion to his purification of his "will to receive" that he attains to the lights and the levels of his Soul (*Neshamah*) that are termed *Nefesh* (Crude Spirit), *Ruah* (Spirit), *Neshamah* (Soul), *Hayyah* (Living) and *Yehidah* (Individual). Whatever level he reaches, the lights of that level assist him in his purification process and thus he ascends through all the levels until he succeeds in reaching the delights of the ultimate purpose that is contained in the Thought of Creation. In this connection the Zohar comments (in *Noah*, 63) on the phrase "He who wishes to be purified is helped", by asking "How is he helped?" and then answers "With a holy Soul (*Neshamah*)". For it is impossible to arrive at the purification that is desirable to the Thought of Creation without the assistance of all the levels of Crude Spirit (*Nefesh*), Spirit (*Ruah*), Soul (*Neshamah*), Living (*Hayyah*) and Individual (*Yehidah*) of the Soul (*Neshamah*), as we have already explained.

You should know also that the Crude Spirit (*Nefesh*), Spirit (*Ruah*), Soul (*Neshamah*), Living (*Hayyah*) and Individual (*Yehidah*) of which we have spoken, are five parts into which the whole of existence is divided. However, whatever is true of the whole is also true of each of the individual components, even the most minute of them. For example, even in the Inanimate aspect of the spiritual world of Making alone, it is necessary to attain the five aspects of Crude Spirit (*Nefesh*), Spirit (*Ruah*), Soul (*Neshamah*), Living (*Hayyah*) and Individual (*Yehidah*) which we related to the five general aspects of Crude Spirit (*Nefesh*), Spirit (*Ruah*), Soul (*Neshamah*), Living (*Hayyah*) and Individual (*Yehidah*), because it is impossible to attain to the light of the Inanimate of the world of Making without the four parts that have been mentioned. Thus, no man of Israel is able to exempt himself from occupying himself with all of them, each in accordance with his own capability. He must therefore occupy himself with the study of the Torah and with the performance of the *Mitzvot* with the proper concentration so as to receive the aspect of the Spirit (*Ruah*) in the amount that is appropriate for him. He must also occupy himself with the study of the esoteric mysteries of the Torah according to his capabilities so as to receive the aspect of Soul (*Neshamah*) in the amount that is appropriate for him. Similarly he *must* occupy himself with the *underlying reasons* for the *Mitzvot*, for it is impossible for even the smallest light in the holy existence to be complete without them.

CHAPTER 15

DECLINE OF SPIRITUALITY — ITS ANTIDOTE

You should have come to understand from what has just been stated that the clouds of darkness that overwhelmed our generation, which cannot be compared to any of the tragedies which have struck our people in the past, came about because even those who served the Lord refrained from occupying themselves with the *esoteric mysteries* of the Torah. Maimonides, of blessed memory, once gave a very true analogy for this situation. He wrote that if a line of a thousand blind people should walk along the road but they have at their head at least one person who **has** sight, they can all be sure that they will be going on the right path and that they will not stumble into traps or snares since they are following the man with vision at their head. However, should but this one man be lacking, there is no doubt that they would all stumble over anything in their path and tumble headlong into a dark abyss. The situation of our generation is very similar to this. Had but at least those who were actually serving the Almighty also occupied themselves with the *inner truths* of the Torah, then the whole generation would have followed them and all would then have been sure not to stumble. However, if even those who serve the Almighty remove themselves from this branch of wisdom, it will not be surprising that the whole generation will stumble and fall because of them. To my deep sorrow, I cannot go into this matter at greater length.

However, I believe that the reason for this was that there has been a general decline of belief in God, and in particular, of belief in the sublime saints, the outstanding scholars of all history. For the books of Kabbalah and also the Zohar contain many physical analogies, thus all became afraid that the rewards to be gained in studying might be lost, for, heaven forbid, one might come to be corrupted into transgressing the prohibition against making graven images or likenesses of God. It is this fear that prompted me to write a commentary, first of all on the Ari of blessed memory and now on the holy Zohar, in which I remove all foundations for this fear. For I have fully explained the spiritual analogy of everything, and abstracted it all from any physical imagery beyond time and beyond place so as to enable the entire common people of Israel to study the book of the Zohar and so warm themselves by its holy light. I called this commentary "The Ladder"* to demonstrate that the function of my commentary is the same as that of a ladder; when there is a high-level room in front of one, full of all manner of good things, all that is needed is a ladder to climb up to it and then all the goodness of the world will be within one's reach. However, a ladder serves no end in itself, that is to say that if one should rest upon one of the rungs of the ladder and not enter into the high-level room, one's intention will not be carried out. The same is true of my commentary on the Zohar, for words have not yet

* This is a 21 volume commentary on the entire zohar. (available at the present time in Hebrew only).

been invented that will completely convey the deep meanings of the text.

So what I have done in this commentary of mine is to provide a path and an introduction for any person who should wish by means of it to attempt to delve into the holy Zohar itself. Only then will my intention have been achieved.

CHAPTER 16

AUTHORSHIP OF THE ZOHAR

As for the question of who was the author of the holy Zohar, everyone who has been familiar with the Zohar, by which I mean whoever has understood what is written in it, have all been unanimous in maintaining that its author was the godly man of the Mishnaic period Rabbi Shimeon bar Yohai. However, many of those who are distant and far removed from this branch of wisdom have expressed doubts on this point, and on the basis of facts that were invented by those who opposed this branch of wisdom have tended to maintain that the authorship of the Zohar is to be attributed to the Kabbalist Rabbi Moses de Leon, of blessed memory, or someone else of the same period. As for myself, from the day that I have been enabled, by means of the light of the Almighty, to peruse this holy book it never entered my mind to investigate its authorship. The reason for this is simple. The contents of the book caused my mind to conjure up the cherished excellence of the Mishnaic authority Rabbi Shimeon bar Yohai incalculably more than any of the other holy Rabbis who are quoted in the Mishnah. However, had it been absolutely clear to me that the author was someone else, Rabbi Moses de Leon of blessed memory for example, then I would have been constantly aware of the excellence of Rabbi Moses de Leon of blessed memory more than any of the Rabbis of the Mishnah period including Rabbi Shimeon bar Yohai. However, because of the depth of the wisdom in the book, had I found clear proof that its author was one of the forty eight prophets, this would have been more acceptable to me than to attribute it to one of the Rabbis of the Mishnah period. It would be even more acceptable to me had I proof that our teacher Moses received it on Mount Sinai from the Almighty Himself, then I would be truly at rest; for this work is really fitting to be His. However, since I have had the merit to compile a commentary that should prove adequate for whoever wishes to understand some of what is written in the book, I think I am hereby exempted from entering into an investigation on this subject. For no student of the Zohar could ever be satisfied with the possibility that its author could be of lesser rank than the Mishnaic authority, the holy Rabbi Shimeon bar Yohai.

CHAPTER 17

REVELATION OF KABBALAH — WHY NOW

All of this necessarily raises the question, why was the Zohar not revealed to the earlier generations who were without doubt on a higher plane than the later generations and therefore more fitted for it? Together with this a further question must also be asked: Why was a commentary on the Zohar not revealed to any of the Kabbalists before the Ari of blessed memory? Even more surprising than this is, why no commentary on the words of the Ari of blessed memory, or even on the Zohar itself, has appeared from the time of the Ari of blessed memory right up to our own time — (see further my introduction to the book *Panim Masbirot*). The question must then be asked "Is my generation suitable?" (for such a commentary to be written now). However, the answer must be that our world, during the six thousand years of its duration, is like one *Partzuf* (countenance) which is divided into three parts, a head consisting of *Hochmah* (wisdom), *Binah* (intelligence) and *Da'at* (knowledge); a middle consisting of *Hesed* (mercy), *Gevurah* (judgement) and *Tiferet* (beauty); and an end consisting of *Netzah* (lasting endurance), *Hod* (majesty) and *Yesod* (foundation). In this connection our Rabbis of blessed memory stated "In the first two thousand years there is chaos, the next two thousand years are for Torah, and the period of the last two thousand years is the Messianic era"

(*Sanhedrin*, 97a). For in the first two thousand years, which are the aspect of the head and of *Hokhmah* (wisdom), *Binah* (intelligence) and *Da'at* (knowledge), the lights were very few and they were considered as the aspect of a head without a body which contains only the lights of the Crude Spirit (*Nefesh*). Vessels are completely the opposite to lights, it is the general rule in the case of vessels that the primary vessels grow in every *Partzuf* (countenance) right from the outset, whereas with lights it is the opposite, it is the lower lights that are the first that become clothed in the *Partzuf* (countenance). Thus wherever there are to be found only the highest vessels, namely the vessels of *Hokhmah* (wisdom), *Binah* (intelligence) and *Da'at* (knowledge), then only the lowest of the lights, the lights of the Crude Spirit (*Nefesh*), descend to be clothed there. This should explain the saying of our Sages that the first two thousand years were the aspect of chaos.

During the second two thousand years of the world, which were the aspect of *Hesed* (mercy), *Gevurah* (judgement) and *Tiferet* (beauty) of the vessels, the light of the Spirit (*Ruah*) descended and clothed itself in the world, this was the 'secret' (*Sod*) of Torah; they therefore described these middle two thousand years as the years of Torah. As for the last two thousand years they are the *Netzah* (lasting endurance), *Hod* (majesty), *Yesod* (foundation) and *Malkhut* (kingdom) of the vessels, and therefore at this time the greatest of the lights — the light of the Soul (*Neshamah*) — becomes clothed in the world; and these years are the years of the Messianic era. Similarly in the case of every individual *Partzuf* (countenance) which is in the vessels of *Hokhmah* (wisdom), *Binah* (intelligence) and *Da'at* (knowledge), and *Hesed* (mercy), *Gevurah* (judgement) and *Tiferet* (beauty) extending to its breast, the lights remain covered and only begin to radiate their manifest favours — by which is meant the manifestation of the illumination of the sublime wisdom — only from the breast downwards; that is to say in its *Netzah* (lasting enduring), *Hod* (majesty), *Yesod* (foundation) and *Malkhut* (kingdom). It is for this reason that before the vessels of *Netzah* (lasting endurance), *Hod* (majesty), *Yesod* (foundation) and *Malkhut* (kingdom) that are in the *Partzuf* (countenance) of the world commenced becoming manifest, that is to say in the final two thousand years, the wisdom of the Zohar and the wisdom of the Kabbalah in particular was hidden from the world. However, during the period of the Ari of blessed memory, when the time of the completion of the vessels from the breast downwards was approaching, the illumination of the sublime wisdom was made manifest by the godly soul of Rabbi Isaac Luria of blessed memory who was prepared to receive this great light. Thus he revealed the principal points of the Zohar and also of the wisdom of the Kabbalah, to the extent that he outshone all of those who preceeded him. However, since these vessels were not yet fully complete (the Ari of blessed memory died in 5332), the world was not yet worthy that all of his words should be disclosed. Thus his words were only known to an illustrious few who were not permitted to reveal them to the world. However, since in our generation we are now approaching the end of the final two thousand years, permission has been granted to reveal his words and also the words of the Zohar to the world. Thus from our time on, the words of the Zohar will gradually be revealed, more and more each time, until there will be revealed the entire amount that is in the purpose of the Almighty.

You should now understand from this that the earlier generations were much superior to the later generations, for there is a general rule concerning the *Partzufim* (countenances) of the worlds and of the Souls (*Neshamot*) that whatever is purer will be the first to be refined to the *Partzuf* (countenance). Therefore, the vessels of *Hokhmah* (wisdom), *Binah* (intelligence) and *Da'at* (knowledge) of the world and also of the Souls (*Neshamot*) were refined first. Thus the Souls (*Neshamot*) of the first two thousand years were by far the highest. Yet despite this, they were still not able to receive a structure of complete light because of the fact that the lower parts of the world were lacking, as were parts of themselves as well, namely *Hesed* (mercy), *Gevurah* (judgement), *Tiferet* (beauty) and *Netzah* (lasting endurance), *Hod* (majesty), *Yesod* (foundation) and *Malkhut* (kingdom). Thus afterwards, during the middle two thousand years when the vessels of *Hesed* (mercy), *Gevurah* (judgement) and *Tiferet* (beauty) were refined into the world, and similarly some of the Souls (*Neshamot*), the Souls (*Neshamot*) were in their own right a very positive factor indeed for the level of the vessels of *Hesed* (mercy), *Gevurah* (judgement) and *Tiferet* (beauty) is very close to the level of *Hokhmah* (wisdom), *Binah* (intelligence) and *Da'at* (knowledge). Yet despite all this, the lights are still covered in the world due to the fact that the vessels from the breast downwards are still missing from the world, as are the Souls (*Neshamot*) from this level. Therefore, in this age even though the essence of these Souls (*Neshamot*) is the lowest of all existence, for they have as yet been unable to become refined into holiness, yet despite this it is they who complete the *Partzuf* (countenance) of the world and the *Partzuf* (countenance) of the totality of the Souls (*Neshamot*) from the aspect of the vessels, and it is only through them that the work can be completed. For once the vessels of *Nezah* (lasting endurance), *Hod* (majesty) and *Yesod* (foundation) have been completed and all the vessels — that is to say the head and the middle and the end — are now to be found in the *Partzuf* (countenance), then the completed structures of the lights will be extended, in the head and in the middle and in the end, to those that are fitting for them, that is to say to the whole and complete aspects of Crude Spirit (*Nefesh*), Spirit (*Ruah*) and Soul (*Neshamah*), as was explained previously. Thus it is only after these lower Souls (*Neshamot*) have been completed that the upper lights can become revealed and not before.

This question has in fact already been treated in the Talmud (*Berakhot*, 20) by our Sages of blessed memory: "Rav Pappa said to Abbaye 'How is it that miracles were performed for the former generations yet miracles are not performed for us?' It cannot be because of their superiority in study, because in the years of Rav Yehudah the whole of their studies was confined to the order of *Nezikin* (the fourth of the six books of the *Mishnah*) whereas we study all six orders. In fact when Rav Yehudah came to the tractate of *Uktzin* he used to say 'I see here all the difficulties raised by Rav and Shmuel'; whereas, we possess thirteen versions of the tractate of *Uktzin*. Yet when Rav Yehudah drew off one of his shoes (before fasting for rain) rain used to start falling immediately, whereas we torment ourselves and cry loudly yet no notice is taken of us'. Abbaye replied 'The former generations were ready to sacrifice their lives for the sanctification of the name of

God'." From this it can be seen that even though it was clear to Rav Pappa, who asked the question, and to Abbaye who answered it, that the earlier generations were superior to them, yet from the aspect of Torah and of wisdom Rav Pappa and Abbaye were superior to the earlier generations. It has thus been explicitly demonstrated that even though the earlier generations were superior to the later generations from the aspect of the essence of their Souls (*Neshamot*), the reason being that what was the most pure was the first to be refined to come into the world, however, as for the aspect of the wisdom of the Torah every generation sees more of it disclosed. The reason for this is that since the general overall structure is only completed by those that come last, the more complete lights become extended to them even though their essence is of a much lower rank.

It may well be asked that if what has just been stated is true, why is it forbidden to disagree with the earlier authorities in matters of revealed Torah? However, this question is not pertinent, since it must be borne in mind that the opposite is true for whatever is related to the practical aspects of the *Mitzvot*, for in this aspect the earlier generations were more complete than the later generations because the practical aspects are derived from the holy vessels of the *Sefirot*, whereas the esoteric mysteries (*sod*) of the Torah and the underlying reasons for the *Mitzvot* are derived from the lights which are in the *Sefirot*. By now you should know that the vessels go in an opposite direction to the lights, that is to say that in the case of the vessels, the higher ones are the first to develop; it therefore follows that the earlier generations were more complete in the practical aspects of Torah than the later generations. Whereas in the case of the lights it is the lower ones that enter first and therefore the lower ones are more complete in the matter of the lights than the earlier generations.

CHAPTER 18

INTERNAL AND EXTERNAL
PARTS OF CREATION

You should also know that everything in existence consists of an inner part and an external part. In the case of the world, the people of Israel — the descendants of Abraham, Isaac and Jacob — are considered as the inner part of the world, and the seventy nations are considered as the external part of the world. Similarly, Israel itself contains an inner part consisting of those who fully serve the Almighty, and an external part consisting of those who do not devote themselves to the service of the Almighty. There is also amongst the nations of the world an inner part consisting of the righteous non-Jews of the world, and an external part consisting of those among the nations who are crude and inflict damage. Similarly, those of the people of Israel who serve the Almighty can be divided into an inner part who succeed in understanding the Soul (*Neshamah*) of the innermost parts of the Torah and of its esoteric mysteries (*sod*), and the external part who are occupied only with the practical parts of the Torah. Similarly, every single Jew may be divided into two parts, an inner part which consists of the aspect of Israel that is within him — which is the 'secret' (*sod*) of the point in his heart — and an external part which is the aspect of the non-Jew that is within him, which is his physical body. However, even the aspects of the non-Jewish parts in him are considered to be similar to that of converts to Judaism, for since they are closely attached to the inner parts they are very similar to righteous converts to Judaism who have come and attached themselves to the community of Israel.

Thus when a Jew strengthens and values the aspect of his inner part — which is the aspect of Israel in him — more than his exterior part — which is the aspect of the nations of the world that is within him — that is to say when he expends the greater part of his effort and energy to develop and elevate the aspect of the inner part that is within him for the benefit of his Soul (*Nefesh*), and only expends the minimal effort that is absolutely necessary for the survival of the aspect of the nations of the world that is within him — that is to say for his bodily needs — and thus comes to observe that which is written in the *Misnah* (*Avot*, 1) "Make your Torah fixed and your work part-time", then through these actions of his, he will also be having an effect on the internal and external parts of the whole world so that the people of Israel will rise higher and higher in their perfection, and the nations of the world — who are the exterior aspect of the world — will recognize and acknowledge the true worth of the people of Israel. However, if the opposite should happen, heaven forbid, and an individual Jew should fortify and value the aspect of his exterior — which is the aspect of the nations of the world that is within him — more than the aspect of Israel that is within him and thus comes to fulfil the words of the Torah (*Deuteronomy*, 28:43) "The stranger that is in the midst of you..." — that is to say the exterior part of you — "...shall mount up above you higher and higher; and you..." — that is to say the real you, the aspect of Israel that is within you — "...shall descend lower and lower", he will then through his actions be causing the exterior of the world — that is to say the nations of the world — to rise higher and higher and so overcome Israel and bring them down into the dust. He will also be causing the people of Israel — the inner part of the world — to descend, heaven forbid, lower and lower.

You should not be amazed that an individual person should through his actions be able to cause the whole world to ascend or descend, for this is an irrevocable law. You should also know that the general and the particular are as similar to each other as two drops of water, for whatever occurs in the general also occurs in the particular; in fact, the opposite is even more correct, it is the particular components that go to make up whatever is contained in the general. For the general does not become manifest until after the particular components in it have become manifest and then only according to the nature and quality of the particular components. Thus it is obvious that the actions of the individual, each according to his worth, can cause the whole community to go down or go up. This should clarify for you the words of the Zohar in which it says that "It is through occupying themselves with the book of the Zohar and with the true wisdom that they will succeed in emerging from the exile to the complete redemption" (*Tikkunim*, 6). At first sight the connection between the study of the Zohar and the redemption of Israel from the nations of the world is not too apparent.

CHAPTER 19

THE BODY AND SOUL OF TORAH

From the preceeding explanation it should be perfectly clear that the Torah also has an inner part and an exterior part just like the whole world, and therefore a man who occupies himself with the Torah also contains these two levels. Thus when a man increases his efforts in the direction of the inner part of the Torah and its esoteric mysteries (*sod*), he then becomes a factor in causing the inner part of the world — that is to say Israel — to rise higher and higher in similar proportions above the external part of the world, that is to say above the nations of the world. Then all the nations will acknowledge and recognize Israel's superiority over them so that the prophecy of Isaiah will be fulfilled "And the peoples shall take them, and bring them to their place; and the house of Israel shall possess them in the land of the Lord for servants and for housemaids..." (Isaiah, 14:2). And also the verse "Thus saith the Lord God: Behold, I will lift up My hand to the nations and set up Mine ensign to the peoples, and they shall bring thy sons in their bosom, and thy daughters shall be carried on their shoulders..." However, if the opposite should occur, heaven forbid, and a man from Israel should lower the value of the inner part of the Torah and its esoteric mysteries (*sod*) which deal with the paths of our Souls (*Neshamot*) and their various levels, and also of the rational parts and those pertaining to the underlying reasons for the *Mitzvot*, in comparison with the value of the external parts of the Torah which deal with only the practical aspects. Even if he was from time to time to occupy himself with the inner part of the Torah but then alloting to it only a limited amount of his time during the time which is neither day nor night, as if it were something which was completely super-fluous, heaven forbid — he would hereby be a contributing factor in the lessening of the value and the degredation of the inner part of the world — the people of Israel — and be contributing to the strengthening of the power of the ex-terior part of the world — the nations of the world — over them so that they would despise and degrade the people of Israel and consider Israel as being something which was super-fluous in the world, of which the world has no need, heaven forbid. Furthermore, he would also be contributing to the strengthening of the power of the external parts of the nations of the world over their own inner parts, and thus the meanest among the nations of the world, those who spread damage and destruction throughout the world, will become stronger and stronger and rise above their own inner parts, that is to say over the righteous of the nations of the world, and then they will commit those terrible massacres which our own genera-tion have witnessed with their own eyes, and from which may the Almighty henceforth preserve us! Thus it should be clear to you that the redemption of Israel and the high position of Israel are dependent on the study of the Zohar and of the inner parts of the Torah. The opposite is also true, the des-truction and the low position of the people of Israel have taken place due to their having forsaken the inner parts of the Torah and their having brought it down lower and lower and made it as if it was something that was completely superfluous, heaven forbid.

We shall now bring a passage from the *Tikkunim* which clarifies this, and we shall explain it passage by passage (*Tikun*, 30): "Arise and be stirred for the *Shechinah*, for you have a heart without understanding to know it even though it is in your midst..." The meaning of this is plain.

"And the "secret" (*sod*) of the matter is contained in the verse 'A voice says 'cry out'!' as in the verse 'Cry out now; is there any that will answer you? And to which of the holy ones will you turn?' (*Job*, 5:1). And it replies 'What shall I cry out, all flesh is as grass' — all of them are as cattle that eat grass — 'and all his goodliness is as the flower of the field' — all the goodness that they do they do for themselves". This is understood as follows: and the 'secret' (*sod*) of the matter is as it is written in Isaiah (*Isaiah*, 40:6) "A voice says 'cry out'!", there is a voice that knocks on the heart of every single individual from Israel that he should cry out and pray for the elevation of the holy *Shechinah* which is the totality of the Souls (*Neshamot*) of all Israel (and he brings the verse "cry out now is there any that will answer you?" as a proof that the word 'cry out' has the meaning of prayer). However, the *Shechinah* replies "What shall I cry out?" which means 'I do not have strength to raise myself up from the dust because "all flesh is grass" they are all as cattle which eat grass, that is to say they perform the *Mitzvot* without any understanding just like cattle, "and all its goodliness is as the flower of the field" all the good acts that they do they do for themselves alone, that is to say in performing a *Mitzvah* their intention is not to bring pleasure to their Creator but rather they perform the *Mitzvot* for their own benefit alone.

"And even those who occupy themselves with the Torah, whatever good they do they do for themselves." This means that even the good ones among them who devote their time to occupying themselves with the Torah, do so only for the benefit of themselves and not with the desired intention of giving pleasure to their Creator.

"At that time... a Spirit (*Ruah*) will go and will not return to the world, and this is the spirit of the Messiah". The meaning of this passage is that at that time — referring to the time of the generation of people who have just been described — a spirit will go and will not return to the world, which is the spirit of the Messiah which is supposed to redeem Israel from all their troubles to the complete redemption so that there shall be fulfilled the verse in which it is written "And the earth shall be full of the knowledge of the Lord as the waters cover the sea..." (*Isaiah*, 11:9). However, this spirit departs and does not illuminate the world.

"Woe to those who cause it to disappear from the world so that it will never return, because it is they who cause the Torah to become dry, and they do not desire to make an effort at the wisdom of the Kabbalah". The interpretation of this passage of the *Tikkunim* is as follows: Woe to those men who cause the spirit of the Messiah to disappear from the world so that it is unable to return, for it is they who make the Torah dry, that is to say without any moist drops of knowledge and understanding, for they confine themselves only to the practical parts of the Torah and do not wish to try and understand the wisdom of the Kabbalah so as to know and understand the esoteric mysteries (*sod*) of the Torah and the underlying reasons for the *Mitzvot*.

"Woe to those who cause poverty, war, despoilation, killing and destruction in the world" which means, woe to those who through these actions of theirs are the cause of their being poverty, war, violence, despoilation, slaughter and massacres in the world.

The reason underlying the words in the passage just quoted is to be understood in the light of what we have previously explained. Namely that since those who do occupy themselves with Torah treat their own inner part and the inner part of the Torah contemptuously and set it aside as though it was a subject that was completely superfluous to the world and so only occupy themselves with it at times which are neither day nor night, and then they come to it as blind men groping at a wall, they hereby increase the power of their external parts, that is to say they increase the benefit of their own physical bodies. Similarly they attribute more importance to the external parts of the Torah than to the inner parts. Through these actions of theirs they cause all the external aspects in the world to increase their power over the inner parts that are in the world, each according to its nature. For the external part of the community of Israel, which consists of the ignorant and unlearned amongst them, becomes stronger and comes to eliminate the inner parts of the community of Israel, namely the great authorities of the Torah. Similarly the external parts amongst the nations of the world, namely those amongst them who wreak havoc and destruction, also become stronger and nullify the inner parts among them, namely the righteous of the nations of the world. Similarly the external part of the whole world, namely the nations of the world also become stronger and come to eliminate the people of Israel who are the inner part of the world. And in such a generation all the wielders of destruction amongst the nations of the world raise their heads and desire to destroy and kill principally the people of Israel, which is as it is stated in the Talmud "Retribution comes to the world only on account of Israel" (*Yevamut*, 63). This idea is also contained in the passages from the *Tikkunim* that we just quoted, which clearly state that it is they (those who make the Torah dry) who are the causes of the poverty, war, robbery, killings and massacres in the world.

Since, due to the large number of our sins, we have witnessed with our own eyes what the *Tikkunim* have described, and furthermore we have witnessed that the attribute of justice (*din*) alighted specifically on the best of our people, as the Talmud states "It begins with the righteous first..." (*Baua Kamma*, 60), and from all the glory of the people of Israel in Poland and Lithuania etc. there remain but a few survivors in our holy land. It must therefore now be the duty of those of us who escaped to correct this serious deviation and every one of us who has survived should accept upon himself, with all his soul and with all his might, that henceforth he will strengthen the inner part of the Torah and accord it its rightful place as is due to it because of its being of greater importance than the external parts of the Torah. Then every single one of us will succeed in making his own inner part — which is the aspect of Israel that is within him — which is the needs of his Soul (*Nefesh*), superior to the aspect of his external part, which is the aspect of the nations of the world that is within him, which is the needs of his physical body. This increased strength will then reach the whole community of Israel even to the ignorant and unlearned amongst us so that they will then recognize and acknowledge the excellence and high position of the great Torah authorities of Israel over them, and they will then listen to them and obey them. In the same way the inner part of the nations of the worlds, consisting of the righteous of the nations of the world, will also become stronger and will subdue their external parts, which consist of those who wield destruction. Similarly the inner part of the world — Israel — will grow strong in all its excellence and high position over the external part — the nations of the world. Then all of the nations of the world will recognize and acknowledge the superiority of Israel over them, and they will then fulfill the prophecy contained in Isaiah (*Isaiah*, 14:3) "And the peoples shall take them, and bring them to their places; and the people of Israel shall possess them in the land of the Lord for servants and for handmaids..." And further "... and they shall bring your sons in their bosom, and your daughters shall be carried on their shoulders." What we have explained is also written in the Zohar (*Naso*, page 124) "Through this composition of yours, the book of the Zohar etc., they will go out from exile with mercy." Amen, and so let it be His will.

PART TWO

AN INTRODUCTION TO THE ZOHAR

CHAPTER 1

THE TEN SEFIROT AND
ITS LIMITATIONS

The deep wisdom of the holy Zohar is firmly locked by thousands of keys, and the human language is too limited to be able to convey, fully and truthfully, the explanation of even a single phrase of this book from beginning to end. The commentary I have written on the Zohar is merely intended to be a ladder to assist the inquirer in ascending to the heights of the literal meanings of the words so that from there he will proceed to search and delve into the meaning of the book itself. I have therefore found it necessary to prepare the prospective student with a guide and an introduction on how to understand this book.

First of all you must know that the whole of the Zohar, including the narrative parts, consists entirely of the ten *Sefirot* that are termed *Keter* (crown), *Hokhmah* (wisdom), *Binah* (intelligence), *Hesed* (mercy), *Gevurah* (judgement), *Tiferet* (beauty), *Netzah* (lasting endurance), *Hod* (majesty), *Yesod* (foundation) and *Malkhut* (kingdom), and of combinations of these ten *Sefirot*. In the same way that it is the various combinations of the twenty-two letters of the Hebrew language that are sufficient for us to bring to light any object of wisdom, similarly, it is the sets and combinations of sets of these ten *Sefirot* that are sufficient to bring to light all the wisdom that is to be found in the Zohar. However, there are three limits or boundaries beyond which one should be careful not to overstep when studying this book. I will first of all enumerate them and then proceed to explain them more fully.

1. You should know that there are four categories of rational classification (a) Matter, (b) Form that is contained in matter, (c) Abstract form, (d) Essence. The ten *Sefirot* are to be similarly classified, as I will explain later. However, you must know that the Zohar does not deal with the essence or even with the abstract form of the ten *Sefirot*, but it only deals with the matter part of them and also with the form part while it is in a state of being clothed by matter.

2. You should know that the totality of the divine existence that is connected with the creation of the Souls (*Neshamot*) and with ways of sustaining them, is differentiated for us into three aspects, consisting of (a) The "Endless", blessed be He; (b) The world of Emanation; (c) The three Worlds of *Beriah* (Creation), *Yetzirah* (Formation) and *Asiah* (Making). However, you must know that the Zohar deals only with the three worlds of Creation, Formation, and Making. But the "Endless" and the World of Emanation are dealt with only inasmuch as they pertain to that which these three worlds receive from them, but the Zohar never deals with the Blessed "Endless" and the world of Emanation as categories on their own.

3. You should know that in each one of the three worlds of Creation, Formation and Making there are three aspects; (a) The ten *Sefirot* that constitute the Godliness that illuminates each world, (b) The Souls (*Neshamot*) and Spirits (*Ruhot*) and the Crude Spirits (*Nefashot*) of mankind, (c) All

else that exists in each of the worlds and which is denoted under the terms "Angels", "Garments" and "Halls"—all possessing innumerable parts. However, you should understand that even though the Zohar goes into lengthy explanations of all the parts of each world, the principal words of the Zohar are always centered on the aspects of the human Souls (*Neshamot*) of each world. When it goes into explanations of the other aspects it does so merely so as to clarify what the Souls (*Neshamot*) receive from them. However, the Zohar does not devote even a single word to anything that is not connected with that which the Souls (*Neshamot*) receive. Therefore, when studying the Zohar your mind should be directed only towards understanding what pertains to the receiving of the Soul (*Neshamah*).

These three limits are to be strictly observed. If a student should not be wary of them but should interpret some of the words of the Zohar beyond these limits he will immediately become very confused. I have therefore deemed it necessary to explain these limits in greater length so that they should be understood by all.

You should know by now that there are ten *Sefirot* that are termed *Hokhmah* (wisdom), *Binah* (intelligence), *Tiferet* (beauty) and *Malkhut* (kingdom) whose root is *Keter* (crown). [They add up to ten because *Tiferet* (beauty) includes the other six *Sefirot*; *Hesed* (mercy), *Gevurah* (judgement), *Tiferet* (beauty), *Netzah* (lasting endurance), *Hod* (majesty) and *Yesod* (foundation)]. This fact should be borne in mind whenever the ten *Sefirot* are mentioned as being *Hokhmah* (wisdom), *Binah* (intelligence), *Tiferet* (beauty) and *Malkhut* (kingdom).

These ten *Sefirot* generally include all the four worlds of

Emanation, Creation, Formation, and Making, for the world of Emanation is the *Sefirah Hokhmah* (wisdom), the world of Creation is the *Sefirah Binah* (intelligence), the world of Formation is the *Sefirah Tiferet* (beauty), and the world of Making is the *Sefirah Malkhut* (kingdom). However, not only do all of these four worlds contain individually all of the ten *Sefirot*, but even the most minute part of each world contains all of the ten *Sefirot*, as we explained in the Preface to the Zohar (page 50).

CHAPTER 2

THE FOUR COLORS

The Zohar gave these ten *Sefirot*, *Hokhmah* (wisdom), *Binah* (intelligence), *Tiferet* (beauty) and *Malkhut* (kingdom) the analogy of four colors: white for the *Sefirah Hokhmah* (wisdom), red for the *Sefirah Binah* (intelligence), green for the *Sefirah Tiferet* (beauty) and black for the *Sefirah Malkhut* (kingdom). This analogy is to be understood by means of an example of a mirror that has four different glass panes and each of the panes is colored with one of these four different colors. Although only one light enters the mirror, when it reflects through the glass panes it becomes colored, and thus this light becomes transformed into four different colored lights, a white light, a red light, a green light, and a black light. Similarly, the light that is in all of the *Sefirot*, from the top of the world of Emanation to the end of the world of Making, is pure Godliness and absolutely One, but its division into the ten *Sefirot Hokhmah* (wisdom), *Binah* (intelligence), *Tiferet* (beauty) and *Malkhut* (kingdom) occurs by means of the vessels that are termed *Hokhmah* (wisdom), *Binah* (intelligence), *Tiferet* (beauty) and *Malkhut* (kingdom). For each vessel is like a pure filter through which the divine light passes through to that which receives it, thus each vessel transforms this light into a different color. The vessel of *Hokhmah* (wisdom) which is in the world of Emanation transmits a white light, that is to say a colorless light. This is because the vessel of the world of Emanation is just as the light itself, and so the divine light does not become changed by it when it passes through it. This is the "secret" (*Sod*) of what the Zohar states concerning the world of Emanation. "He, His vitality and His Substance are One". Therefore, the light of the world of Emanation is distinctive as a white light. This is not the case for the vessels of the worlds of Creation, Formation and Making. When the light passes through them to that which receives it, it does become changed. Thus the analogy of a red light is used for *Binah* (intelligence) which is the world of Creation, and the analogy of a green light is used for *Tiferet* (beauty) which is the world of Formation, and the analogy of a black light is used for the *Sefirah Malkhut* (kingdom) which is the world of Making.

Apart from what has just been stated there is a very significant allusion that is contained in the comparing of the *Sefirot* with these four colors. For the supernal lights are termed *Sepher* (book), as it is written, "And He created His world with three uses of a *Sepher*, with a book (*Sepher*), a scribe (*Sopher*) and a story (*Sippur*)" (*Sepher Yetzirah*, 1:1). We also find "And the heavens shall be rolled together as a book (*Sepher*)" (Isaiah 34:4). The wisdom in any book is not made manifest through the white part of it but only through the colors, that is to say through the ink, for it is through the ink that the letters in the book combined with the wisdom they contain reach the student. One generally finds that in the writing of books it is these three kinds of ink that are used, namely red, green, and black. Similarly the world of Emanation — which is the *Sefirah Hokhmah* (wisdom) and consists entirely of the divineness — is similar to the white part of the book, that is to say we are unable to grasp any part of it. The only parts of the heavenly book that are revealed are in the *Sefirot Binah* (intelligence), *Tiferet* (beauty) and *Malkhut* (kingdom), which are the three worlds of Creation, Formation, and Making, since they are the ink in the heavenly book (*Zohar*). And seeing that it is by means of the three kinds of ink that we have mentioned that the letters are made visible, therefore, the divine light is made manifest to those that receive it only through these three worlds. However, one must be careful to distinguish the fact that it is the white part of the book that is the principal carrier of the book, and all of the letters are "carried" on the white part of the book. In fact were it not for the white part the letters could not exist nor would any of the wisdom they contain be disclosed. Similarly the world of Emanation — which is the *Sefirah Hokhmah* (wisdom) — is the principal carrier of the wisdom that is manifested through the three worlds of Creation, Formation and Making; this is the "secret" (*Sod*) of the verse "All of it didst Thou make in wisdom (*Hokhmah*)."*

It is to this that we were referring previously when we stated, with reference to the second limit, that the Zohar never describes the world of Emanation as it is by itself, since it is to be compared to the white part of the book, but it only speaks of it with reference to its radiating light into the three worlds of Creation, Formation and Making. The reason for this is that these three worlds are to be compared to the ink and the letters of the book. This process occurs in two ways.

---

* (Psalms, 104:24)

The three worlds of Creation, Formation and Making may either receive the radiated light of the world of Emanation in their own positions so that the light is refracted to them quite considerably as it passes through the "barrier" that is under the world of Emanation so that it is distinguished as to illumine only the vessels of Emanation. Or the worlds of Creation, Formation and Making may ascend above the "barrier" to the location of the *Sefirot Binah* (intelligence), *Tiferet* (beauty) and *Malkhut* (kingdom) of Emanation and there become clothed in the world of Emanation, so that they receive the light in the place from which it radiates. (This is explained in the Introduction to the Wisdom of the Kabbalah, page 154).*

However, this analogy is by no means perfect. For in a book of wisdom of this world both the white part and the ink of the lettering contain no life in them, and the manifestation of the wisdom that is revealed through them does not occur within these substances but only outside them, that is to say in the brain of the student who reads them. This is not the case for the four worlds of Emanation, Creation, Formation and Making which constitute the book of heaven, for all of the "brains" (*Mohin*) in the spiritual and physical exis-

---

* This might be compared to a candle that is lit and placed in a position whereby the direct rays of the sun are refracted by a curtain. While the light of the sun obviously illuminates the other side of the curtain it is of a lesser quality, thereby enabling the flame to be distinguishable from the rays of the sun. This is what is alluded to when we refer to the "light being refracted through the barrier that is under the World of Emanation", enabling the vessels of Emanation (or to what we refer as the flame and candle) to be distinguished. However, were we to take the same candle and place it within the direct rays of the sun, the vessel or candle itself would remain the same, but the flame would not be apparent. This is what is meant by the vessels ascending above the "barrier".

tence are to be found in them and extend from them. You should therefore know that the white part of it, which is the carrier of the book, is itself the wisdom in the book, and it is the three different colors of ink that explain this wisdom.

CHAPTER 3

THE FOUR CATEGORIES

We shall now explain the four various categories of rational classification that were mentioned previously with reference to the first limit, (a) Matter, (b) Form that is contained in matter, (c) Abstract form, (d) Essence. We will first explain them with reference to the tangible objects of this world. For example, when one describes a man as being a strong man or an honest man or a false man etc., the following aspects have been described: (a) his matter, that is to say his physical body; (b) the form that is clothed in his matter, that is to say his strength, his honesty, or his falseness; (c) pure abstract form, that is to say the form of the abstract concepts of strong, honest and false when they are abstracted from the matter of the man; one is then able to comprehend these three forms by themselves unencased by any matter or body, that is to say, one will then be able to comprehend the attributes of strength, truth, and falsehood and thus be able to distinguish between the positive and the negative aspects of them when they have been abstracted from all matter;* (d) the essence of the man.

You should know that the fourth category — the pure essence of a man that is abstracted from all matter — cannot

---

* See p. 61.

be comprehended by our understanding. For our five senses and our imagination can only transmit to us the manifestations of the activities of the essence. For example, our sense of sight can transmit to us only shadows of the manifest essence through the impressions caused by the light. Similarly, the sense of hearing is merely the force that an essence impels when it strikes against the atmosphere, then the atmosphere that is impelled by this force strikes against our eardrums, and then we are able to hear that there is an essence near us. The sense of smell consists merely of the air that is expelled from an essence and strikes our smelling glands and so we come to smell it. Taste is also similar, it is merely the consequence of an essence having contact with our tasting glands. Consequently, all of these four senses only transmit to us the manifestations of actions that are caused by an essence but nothing of the essence itself. This is even true for the sense of feeling which is the most powerful of the senses and which distinguishes between hot and cold, between solids and liquids, for these qualities are merely manifestations of actions that have taken place within the essence and are also merely states of the essence at particular times. The hot can be made cold, the solid can be transformed by means of heating into liquids, the liquids can be transformed into gases which are completely indistinguishable to all the five senses, and yet the essence will still be contained in them for you can again transform these gases into liquids, then the liquids into a solid substance. It should thus be clear to you that the five senses will never reveal any essence to us but only states that happen to it and manifestations of activities that derive from it. It is also well know that what is not felt by our senses cannot enter our imagination. That which cannot enter the imagination can never enter the realm of thought and so we can never comprehend it. Therefore, our thoughts can never grasp any essence. Furthermore, we can never even know our own essence. I feel and know that I occupy space in the world, that I am solid and warm, that I think and other similar manifestations of the activities of my essence. However, should you ask me what is my essence from which all these manifestations derive, I should be unable to answer. For providence has prevented us from comprehending the essence, we can only comprehend the manifestations and appearances of actions that are derived from the essences.

As for the first category, namely matter, which consists of the manifestations of the actions that are manifested from every essence, we can comprehend these completely. They explain to us the essence that is in the matter so adequately that we suffer no loss at all through our inability to comprehend the essence as it is by itself. We do not feel that we lack something because of this, in the same way that we do not feel that we lack a sixth finger on our hands. Thus the comprehension of matter — which is the manifestation of an essence — is sufficient for all that is needed in order to understand our own existence and to understand the existence of all that surrounds us.

The second category — form encased in matter — is also a clear and satisfactory concept, for we are able to comprehend it from actual experiences of the behavior of all matter. It is from this category that we derive all the higher comprehension that we possess which may be depended upon.

The third category is absolute form. That is to say after a

form is made manifest to us, while it is still clothed in matter, our imagination possesses the power to strip it from the matter and to comprehend it abstracted from all matter. For example, the virtues and good qualities that are brought in moralistic books, for when we speak of the qualities truth, falsehood, anger and strength and similar qualities, we speak of them when they are abstracted from all matter. Then we give them a positive or negative value even when they are in an abstract form. You should know that this third classification is not used by careful thinkers because it is impossible to depend on it one hundred per cent, for when qualities are considered in an abstract form, mistakes are likely to be made. For example, a man of ideal moral principles, who does not happen to observe religious practise, may be so occupied with the virtue truth in its abstract form, that were he able to save some people from death by telling them something untrue, he may well decide that even if the whole world were to plunge to destruction he will never intentionally utter a false word. However, this is not the view of the Torah according to which there is nothing which the duty of saving an endangered life does not override (*Yoma*, 8a). Moreover, if this person were able to perceive the forms of truth and falsehood at the time when they became clothed in matter he would then understand that the meaning they then acquired depended on their inherent capability to either bring benefit or do harm to matter; that is to say, that it was after the world had had much experience of these forms and seen the amount of destruction and damage that men of falsehood caused through their speaking falsehood, and the amount of benefit that men of truth brought by constraining themselves to speaking only words of truth, that all agreed that there was no virtue that was superior to the quality of truth, and that there was no evil greater than the quality of falsehood. If this idealist would understand this point, he would then surely agree with the view of the Torah and conclude that the speaking of falsehood to save the life of even one person from death is far superior to all the greatness and excellence of abstract truth. Thus, there is absolutely no certainty in those concepts of the third classification, namely abstract forms;* this is even more true of those abstract forms which have never been clothed in any matter at all, for concepts such as these are a mere waste of time.

After you have understood these four classifications namely, tangible objects into matter, form that is contained in matter, abstract form and essence, it should be clear that the fourth category consisting of essence cannot be comprehended by us at all, and that the third category consists of a concept which is liable to lead to mistakes being made. Thus it is only the first and the second categories, consisting of matter and form that is clothed in matter, that Divine Providence has enabled us to understand clearly and fully. And with the assistance of these categories you should also be able to comprehend the existence of spiritual substances that are in the sublime worlds of Emanation, Creation, Formation and Making. For

---

* It should be understood that physical action is motivated by metaphysical forces such as love, hate, happiness and sadness. While these metaphysical forces cannot be understood in their abstract form by themselves, yet in our relationship to others it becomes clear. This is what we consider to be essence. That metaphysical concept which is revealed by physical action, which without the development or manifestation of physical behaviour, one could never discern or determine ones' own essence. But one must always be aware of the fact, that to identify the essence itself still remains beyond comprehension.

there is not even a minute part of these worlds that cannot be classified into one of these four categories. For example, if you were to consider a part of the world of Creation, you would find vessels there that are red in color, by means of which the light of Creation passes to created beings, as we explained previously. The vessel in the world of Creation which is red in color is the aspect of matter or substance which is the first category. Even though it is merely a color that serves to manifest the activity of that which is contained in the substance, we are incapable of understanding the essence itself, but only the manifestations of the activity which proceeds from the essence. It is the manifestation of this activity that we term by the name of substance, or matter, or body, or vessel (see page 74). The divine light that is clothed in and passes through the red coloring is the form which is clothed in the matter, which is the second category. For the light itself is manifested in the aspect of a red light which demonstrates its being clothed in and its illuminating through the substance, which is the aspect of the physical body and of the matter, as has been previously explained, and thus is the red coloring. However, if you should wish to abstract the divine light from the substance, which is the red coloring, and then wish to consider it on its own without its being clothed in substance, this would then belong to the third category, namely form that is abstracted from matter, a category which is liable to mistakes being made as was explained previously. This category is therefore strictly prohibited for those wishing to understand the sublime worlds, and no real Master of Kabbalah would ever occupy himself with it, let alone any Master of the Zohar. This is even more true for the "essence" of any part of the world of Creation, for we are completely incapable of comprehending the essence at all, even the essence of material substances, how much more the essence of spiritual substances!

Thus you should now be aware of four categories:

1. The vessel of Creation — the 'secret' (*sod*) of the red coloring — which is distinguished as the substance or the matter of the Creation.

2. The divine light that is clothed in the vessel of Creation, which is the form in the substance.

3. The divine light as it is by itself when it is abstracted from the substance of creation.

4. The essence of any single part.

The first limit has now been fully explained, thus it should now be clear that there is not one word in the Zohar that pertains to the third and fourth categories of rational classification, but it limits itself to the first and second categories.

CHAPTER 4

THE SECOND LIMIT

The preceding explanation should also contribute to the understanding of the second limit. You should know that the four categories which we explained in reference to any single part of the world of Creation alone are similarly to be found in all of the worlds of Emanation, Creation, Formation and Making. For the three colorings of red, green and black which are to be found in the three worlds of Creation, Formation and Making, are the aspect of matter or substance. The white coloring, which is the aspect of the world of Emanation, is the form that is clothed in the matter, that is to say, in the three colorings that are termed Creation, Formation and Making. The aspect of the "Endless", when it is by itself, is the 'secret' (*sod*) of the essence; yet, as we said when discussing the first limit, we are completely incapable of comprehending the essence for it is the fourth category that is concealed in all of the substances, even in the substances that are in this world (see page 74). Thus the white coloring as it is by itself unclothed in the three colorings of the Creation, Formation and Making, is form abstracted from matter and thus does not concern us at all. The Zohar does not have anything at all to say about this category. But the Zohar only discusses the first category which consists of the three colorings of Creation, Formation and Making that are considered to be matter, and which are the three *Sefirot Binah* (intelligence), *Tiferet* (beauty) and *Malkhut* (kingdom). It also discussed the second category which consists of the illumination of the Emanation that is clothed in the three colorings of Creation, Formation and Making, that is to say, the light of *Hochmah* (wisdom) that is clothed in the *Sefirot Binah* (intelligence), *Tiferet* (beauty) and *Malkhut* (kingdom), which is then the aspect of form when it is clothed in matter. Thus it is with only these two categories that the Zohar deals, and it does so in many places. Therefore, if the student is not careful to confine and restrict his thoughts and his mind so as to comprehend the words of the Zohar only within the limit of these two categories the whole subject will then become confusing for him, for he will then have extracted the words from their real meaning.

The way in which these four categories have been explained for all the worlds of Emanation, Creation, Formation and Making, is also applicable for each single world, and even for a minute part of any one of these worlds, whether it be at the head of the world of Emanation, or at the end of the world of Making, for as has previously been explained, each part contains in it the *Sefirot Hochmah* (wisdom), *Binah* (intelligence), *Tiferet* (beauty) and *Malkhut* (kingdom). Thus the *Sefirah Hochmah* (wisdom) is the aspect of form, and the *Sefirot Binah* (intelligence), *Tiferet* (beauty) and *Malkhut* (kingdom), are the aspects of matter in which the form is clothed. Thus, these are the first and second categories with which the Zohar deals, but it does not deal with the *Sefirah Hokhmah* (wisdom) when it is abstracted from the *Sefirot Binah* (intelligence), *Tiferet* (beauty) and *Malkhut* (kingdom) which is then form without matter, and certainly not with the essence which is the aspect of the Blessed "Endless" which is contained in every individual part. To sum up, the Zohar does discuss the aspects of *Binah* (intelligence), *Tiferet* (beauty) and *Malkhut* (kingdom) that are contained in every component part, and even in the Emanation. As for the *Keter* (crown) and *Hokhmah* (wisdom) of every part, even in the *Malkhut* (kingdom) of the end of the world of Making, it does not discuss these at all from the aspect of themselves, that is to say, when they are in an abstract form, but only when they are clothed in *Binah* (intelligence), *Tiferet* (beauty) and *Malkhut* (kingdom). Thus the first two limits should now be clear:

1. The Masters of Zohar deal only with matter, or with form that is in matter; this is limit one.

2. Similarly, the Zohar deals only with the worlds of Creation, Formation and Making, or with the illumination of the Emanation in the worlds of Creation, Formation and Making; this is limit two.

CHAPTER 5

THE THIRD LIMIT

We shall now explain the third limit. The Zohar deals with every world from the aspect of the *Sefirot*, which constitute the divineness that illuminates each world, and it also deals with all of the components of the Inanimate, Vegetative, Animal and Human aspects which are the created beings in each world. However, the Zohar directs its attention principally to the Human aspect in each world. I will bring you an example of this from the situation prevailing in this world. It was explained previously (see page 54) that the four species Inanimate, Vegetative, Animal and Human that are to be found in every world, and even in this world, are four parts of the "will to receive". In fact, each of these species contains in itself every one of the four species Inanimate, Vegetative, Animal and Human. A man in this world needs to be nourished and to grow by means of all the four aspects of Inanimate, Vegetative, Animal and Human that exist in this world. Thus a man's food also contains these four aspects which are extended from the four Inanimate, Vegetative, Animan and Human aspects that are contained in the body of every human being. These aspects are as follows:

1. He desires to receive what is absolutely essential for survival.

2. He desires more than what is absolutely necessary for

survival, but these are confined to animal cravings alone.

3. He aspires for human cravings such as status and power.

4. He aspires to acquire rational understanding.

These four aspects are extended to him through the four parts of the "will to receive" that is in him. His desire for that which is absolutely necessary for survival is the aspect of the Inanimate of the "will to receive". The desire for animal lusts is the aspect of the Vegetative of the "will to receive", for these cravings come merely to enlarge and give pleasure to his vessel, which is the flesh of his body. The desire for human cravings is the aspect of the Animal which is in the "will to receive", for these lusts enlarge his spirit (*Ruah*). And his desire to acquire rational understanding is the aspect of the Human of the "will to receive".

Thus you will find that a man receives the first aspect, which consists of what is absolutely necessary for his survival and the second aspect, which consists of those animal lusts that are additional to what is necessary for his survival, from beings that are lower in rank than him, namely from the Inanimate, Vegetative and Animal species. But he receives the third aspect, which consists of the human passions for goals such as status and power, and is nourished in it from his own species who are on equal level with him. As for the fourth aspect of food, namely rational thoughts, he receives these and is nourished in them from an aspect that is higher than him, that is to say from the substance of wisdom and understanding which are both spiritual.

In a similar way you should understand the mutual relationships of the sublime spiritual worlds. For all the worlds are affected by each other from the top downwards. Thus all of the Inanimate, Vegetative, Animal and Human aspects which are in the world of Creation leave their mark on the world of Formation. The Inanimate, Vegetative, Animal and Human aspects of the world of Formation leave their imprint on the Inanimate, Vegetative, Animal and Human aspects of the world of Making. The Inanimate, Vegetative, Animal and Human aspects of the world of Making leave their imprint on the Inanimate, Vegetative, Animal and Human aspects of this world. Now it has been explained previously (see page 54) that the Inanimate aspects in the spiritual worlds are given the name of "Halls" (*Hechalot*), and the Vegetative aspects are there given the name of "Garments" (*Levushim*) and the Animal aspects the name of "Angels"; as for the Human, it is the aspect of the Souls (*Neshamot*) of man which are in that world, and the ten *Sefirot* which are in every world are the divineness. Thus the Souls (*Neshamot*) of men are the centre of every world, and a man is nourished from the entire spiritual existence in each world just as the physical Human aspect is nourished from the entire material existence. Thus he receives the first aspect — which is the "will to receive" that which is absolutely necessary for his survival — from the illumination of the "Halls" (*Hechalot*) and of the "Garments" (*Levushim*) which are there. He receives the second aspect — which consists of the animal luxuries that make his body grow — from the aspect of the "Angels" which are there (see (*Tikkunei Zohar*, *Tikun* 69, page 105, line 32) which are spiritual illuminations that are additional to the amount that is needed for his survival, and which contribute to the enlargening of the spiritual vessels in which his Soul (*Neshamah*) is clothed. Thus he receives the first and second aspects from aspects that are on a lower level than his, namely from the "Halls" (*Hechalot*), the "Garments" (*Levushim*) and the "Angels" which are there, which are all on a lower level than the Souls (*Neshamot*) of human beings. As for the third aspect, which consists of human desires that enlarge a man's spirit (*Ruah*), which he receives in this world from his own kind, he also receives them in that world from his own kind, that is to say from all the Souls (*Neshamot*) that are to be found in that world, for it is by means of these that he enlarges the illumination of the spirit (*Ruah*) of his Soul (*Neshamah*). As for the fourth aspect of the "will", which consists of rational thoughts, he receives this from the *Sefirot* in every world, for it is from these that he receives the aspects of *Hokhmah* (wisdom), *Binah* (intelligence) and *Da'at* (knowledge) for his Soul (*Neshamah*). Thus the Soul (*Neshamah*) of a man that is to be found in every world needs to grow and become more complete from all the aspects that are to be found in each world. This is the third limit that we mentioned. The student must understand that all the worlds of the Zohar, in connection with whatever part of the sublime worlds with which it may be dealing, whether it be dealing with a part of the *Sefirot*, or of the *Souls* (*Neshamot*), or of the "Angels", or of the "Garments" (*Levushim*), or of the "Halls" (*Hechalot*), even though it treats them all as categories on their own, yet its words are principally directed towards the subject of the amount that the aspect of the Soul (*Neshamah*) of a man receives from them and is nourished by them. Thus, in effect, all the words of the Zohar are centered around the needs of the Soul (*Neshamah*). If you attempt to understand all of the Zohar according to this line of thought you will then comprehend it and your path will be smooth and successful.

CHAPTER 6

KABBALISTIC TERMINOLOGY AND CONCEPTS

After having explained these three limits we have yet to explain the physical descriptive terms that are brought in the Zohar in connection with the ten *Sefirot* as, for example; "upper" and "lower", "ascent" and "descent", "diminution" and "expansion", "smallness" and "greatness", "separation" and "binding", the numbers and other similar terms for states which are caused in the ten *Sefirot* by the good or bad actions of human beings of the lower world. Yet at first sight all of this appears very surprising, for is it possible that the divineness should be so effected that it should receive changes such as these because of the effect of human beings of the lower world? You might answer this by saying that these terms do not refer to the divineness itself which is clothed in the *Sefirot* and illuminates them, heaven forbid, but only to the vessels of the *Sefirot*. These are not divineness in themselves but were created as something "new", when the Souls (*Neshamot*) were created, to conceal or reveal the measures of spiritual comprehension that are appropriate to the *Souls* (Neshamot) so as to bring them to the completion of the desired "correction" (*Tikun*). This was described previously (see page 106) by means of the example of a mirror that has four glass panes that are dyed with four different colorings, white, red, green and black. They were also compared to the white in a book and the letters in the book. Yet to say that these terms refer to the vessels would only be possible for the three worlds of Creation, Formation and Making where the vessels of the *Sefirot* are "new" and not divineness. This would be not at all true for the world of Emanation where the vessels of the ten *Sefirot* are totally divine together with the divine light which is in them, as has been stated in the *Tikkunim* "He, His Vitality (*Hayyuhi*) and His Substance (*Garmuhi*) are One". "He" refers to the essence of the *Sefirot* which is the 'secret' (*sod*) of the Blessed "Endless". His "Vitality" (*Hayyuhi*) is the 'secret' (*sod*) of the light which illuminates the *Sefirot*, and which is termed the light of the *Hayyah* (Living), for the whole world of Emanation is the aspect of *Hokhmah* (wisdom), and the light of *Hokhmah* (wisdom) is termed the light of the *Hayyah* (Living), and thus we find *Hiyyuhi* in the *Tikkunim*. "His Substance" (*Garmuhi*) refers to the vessels of the *Sefirot*. Thus all is absolute divinity and unity. Therefore it must be asked, how is it possible to understand the changes that we mentioned that human beings of the lower world cause? There is also another question that must be understood: If everything in that world of Emanation is divine and there are not to be found there any created beings that have been created as "new", how then can one distinguish between the three aspects that are mentioned in the *Tikkunei Zohar* "He, His Vitality (*Hayyuhi*) and His Substance (*Garmuhi*?*" Surely the unity is indivisible?

To understand the answer to these questions it is necessary that you remember that which has been explained previously (see page 117), namely that the Substance of God is the 'secret' (*sod*) of "essence". We are not able to comprehend material essences, even our own essences, thus we are most certainly unable to grasp the essence of God. As for the world of Emanation, it is the 'secret' (*sod*) of form. The three worlds of Creation, Formation and Making are the 'secret' (*sod*) of matter. The illumination of the Emanation in the worlds of Creation, Formation and Making is the 'secret' (*sod*) of form that is clothed in matter.

From this you should understand that the name "Endless" (*Ein Sof* — literally 'no end'), Blessed be He, that we use is by no means the name for the essence of God — may He be praised and praised! — for how can we define or limit with a name or a word that which we are incapable or understanding? Since our imagination and our five senses cannot project to us anything of the aspect of the essence, even in the material world, how is it possible that there should be a thought about it or a word for it? This is surely even more true in the case of God Himself, is it not? But we must understand the name "Endless" (*Ein Sof*), Blessed be He, as it is defined for us by the third limit that we mentioned (see page 64); that all the words of the Zohar are centered around the Souls (*Neshamot*) in such a way that the name "Endless" (*Ein Sof*), Blessed be He, is by no means a term that is applicable to the aspect of God in Himself but only from the aspect of His being that in which all the worlds and all the Souls (*Neshamot*) are contained in the 'secret' (*sod*) of the Thought of Creation. This is according to the aspect of 'the end of an action is contained first in the thoughts'. Thus the Thought is the connection through which the entire creation until the completion of the "correction" (*Tikun*) is connected in Him in the name "Endless" (*Ein Sof*) Blessed be He.

It is this that we termed in our earlier introduction (see page 28) by the name "Phase One" of the Souls (*Neshamot*). For all the Souls (*Neshamot*) then exist in Him — may He be praised! — filled with the pleasure and gentleness to the highest level, will receive all this in practise only at the completion of the "correction" (*Tikun*). This has already been explained fully (see Preface page 25), therefore it will not be repeated here.

However, I shall give you an example for this that is taken from a situation in this world. A man who wishes to build a beautiful house sees in front of him, in his very first thoughts about it, a beautiful house together with all its details just as it will be when it will be completed. After this he draws up a plan for putting this wish into action, and he then gives the details to the workers after having considered which parts will be made of wood or stones or iron and such. Only after this has been done will he start actually building the house until it stands completed as it did in his thoughts at the very beginning. You should know that the aspect of the Blessed "Endless" is the 'secret' (*sod*) of the first thought, for in the Thought of Creation the whole of the Creation was depicted in its first complete state. However, the comparison is imperfect, because for the Almighty, future and present are exactly the same and in Him the Thought completes the action, thus He does not have need of tools to execute the plans as we do; therefore He is in Himself the actual reality. As for the world of Emanation, it is the 'secret' (*sod*) of something like the detailed plan that is formed in the mind which will become manifest later as they begin to actually build the house. Thus you should understand that these two phases, namely the

Thought of Creation which is the Blessed "Endless" and also the considered plan of all the details necessary to actually put the Thought into practise, can by no means have attributed to them the aspect of created beings, for they are still in a potential state and have not yet been put into actual practise. This is very similar to the example of a man and his house, for although he may think of the parts of wood, or of stone, or of iron, that he needs to make when he puts the plan into practise, at present the material that he possesses is only conceptual material, and he does not yet possess any real stones, or real wood, whatsoever. The only difference in the comparison is that in the case of a man, a plan in the mind cannot be considered as having a reality in existence. Whereas a divine Thought has a real existence that is more real by far than the reality of the created beings themselves. This explanation of the 'secret' (*sod*) of the "Endless" (*Ein Sof*) Blessed be He and also of the 'secret' (*sod*) of the world of Emanation should make it clear that whenever they are spoken of, it is only with reference to their connection with the creation of the created beings. All the while they are still merely potential forces. Nothing whatsoever of their substance has yet become manifest; just like the example that we brought of a man who works out a plan to put his thoughts into practise yet he does not possess any real stones, or wood, or iron whatsoever.

The three worlds of Creation, Formation and Making plus the mundane world are the aspect of converting the potential into reality; just like the man who actually begins to build his house and brings wood and stones and workmen until the house is completely built. Thus the divineness that shines through the worlds of Creation, Formation and Making —

in the proportions which the Souls (*Neshamot*) need to receive in order that they will reach their completion — is clothed in the ten *Sefirot Keter* (crown), *Hokhmah* (wisdom), *Binah* (intelligence), *Hesed* (mercy), *Gevurah* (judgement), *Tiferet* (beauty), *Nezah* (lasting endurance), *Hod* (majesty), *Yesod* (foundation of the world) and *Malkhut* (kingdom) which are real vessels as compared with the divineness of the Almighty. That is, they do not consist of divineness but rather they are created as "new" for the needs of the Souls (*Neshamot*).

You should consider well the example that we brought above for then you will find how the three phases of the man who wishes to build a house are all connected to each other by means of a cause and effect relationship. The root of all of these phases is the original thought. There will not be a single part of the plan that his mind will draw up which will not be according to the completed action that he conceived in his original thought. Similarly, everything that is implemented at the time of building will be in accordance with the details that were arranged by him in the plan which he conceived in his mind. You should use this example to comprehend the spiritual worlds, and thus understand that there is not even the slightest "new" matter in the world which does not extend from the Blessed "Endless". That is to say, from the aspect of Phase One of the Souls (*Neshamot*) which are to be found in this Phase in the full perfection that they will be after the completion of the "correction" (*Tikun*). This is derived from the aspect of 'the end of an action is contained in the thought first'. Thus Phase One contains everything which will become manifest right up to the completion of the "correction" (*Tikun*). At the very beginning, this

Phase is extended from the Blessed "Endless" to the world of Emanation, as in the example of the plan that is conceived and is derived from the original thought. From the world of Emanation, each component part extends to the worlds of Creation, Formation and Making — similar to our example in which it is the plan conceived of in the mind that is the source of all the details at the time of their being implemented into reality by the actual building of the house. This extension occurs in such a way that there is not even a small part that is created "new" in this world which does not extend from the Blessed "Endless" from the aspect of Phase One of the Souls (*Neshamot*). It then extends from the Blessed "Endless" to the world of Emanation, that is to say, to the corresponding parts that are related to that which will in actual practise be made as "new" in this world. This "newness" then extends from the world of Emanation to the three worlds of Creation, Formation and Making, where the "newness" becomes manifest in actual practise. There it leaves the aspect of divineness and enters into the aspect of a created being. Then into the worlds of Formation and Making, until it extends to the lower levels of this world. If you understand this well, and you compare it all to the practise that is followed in the building of a house by a human being, you will then reach a full understanding. Thus it is clear that there is not a single "new" thing which comes into existence in the world which does not extend from its general source in the Blessed "Endless" and from its particular source in the world of Emanation, to the worlds of Formation, Creation and Making where it receives the aspect of a created being. Only then does it come into existence in this world. Try to comprehend this well.

CHAPTER 7

CONCEPTUAL CHANGES IN METAPHYSICS

You may now understand that all of these changes that are described as taking place in the world of Emanation are not spoken of in connection with the divineness when He is by Himself, but only in connection with the Souls (*Neshamot*) and with what they receive from the Emanation by way of the three worlds of Creation, Formation and Making. As for the matter of the objective existence of the world of Emanation, it has the relationship of a plan that is conceived in the mind in relation to the original thought, which is the Blessed "Endless"; however, there is not yet to be found in any of the two of them, either in the Blessed "Endless" or in the world of Emanation, any trace of the Souls (*Neshamot*); just as a plan that is conceived in a man's mind about which he may think, yet no real wood or stones or iron whatsoever are present in his brain. For the existence of the Souls (*Neshamot*) only begins to become manifest in the world of Creation. And for this reason the vessels of the ten *Sefirot*, which measure the amounts that are to be transmitted to the Souls (*Neshamot*) in actual practise, are most certainly not divineness but rather they are "new" creations, for changes and numbers are not at all possible in the divineness. Therefore, we attribute three colorings to the vessels of the ten *Sefirot* that are to be found in the worlds of Creation, Formation and Making: they are red, green and black. For it is impossible to even consider that they should be the aspect of divineness, for nothing "new" whatsoever can take place, heaven forbid, in Him. However, the light that is clothed in the ten vessels that are in the worlds of Creation, Formation and Making is divineness and absolute Unity, in which no change whatsoever occurs. Even the light that is clothed in the lowest vessel in the world of Making is absolute divineness in which no change whatsoever can occur, heaven forbid. For the light itself is One, and all the changes that occur in His illumination are brought about by the vessels of the *Sefirot* — that are not divineness — which are generally colored with the three colorings that we mentioned. Then it is from those three colorings that innumerable millions of changes take place.

Yet the vessels of the ten *Sefirot* of Creation, Formation and Making most certainly receive all the details of their changes, even the most minute details, from the world of Emanation. That world is the aspect of the conceptual plan of all the details which will become unfolded according to the order of the actual building of the house in the worlds of Creation, Formation and Making. Thus since the vessels of the *Sefirot Hokhmah* (wisdom), *Binah* (intelligence), *Tiferet* (beauty) and *Malkhut* (kingdom) which are in the worlds of Creation, Formation and Making, receive from the *Sefirot Hokhmah* (wisdom), *Binah* (intelligence), *Tiferet* (beauty) and *Malkhut* (kingdom) that are parallel to them in the world of Emanation, that is to say, from the aspect of the conceptual plan contained there, it therefore follows that all the details of the implementation in practise derive their origins from the details that are contained in the conceptual plan. Therefore, from this aspect we term the vessels of Emanation by the name of the color white, which is in fact not a color at all. However, white is the source of all colors; an example of this can be seen in the white that is contained in a book of wisdom. Although we have no understanding at all of the white part, and the white part of the book does not tell us anything, yet it is the part that carries all of the book of wisdom. For it illuminates every letter outside and inside so that it is the white that gives every letter its particular form. It allots a particular place to every combination of letters to the extent that it would be possible to maintain the opposite to what we stated above, and claim that we are incapable of understanding the substance of the red or green or black letters, but that all of the comprehension that we achieve in the substance of the letters of the book is due to the white part of it. It is the illumination of the white round every letter and inside every letter that creates these colors into forms. Then these forms disclose to us the wisdom contained in the book. This is analogous to the ten *Sefirot* of Emanation; although they are compared to the color white and one cannot perceive in them any number or change or any similar term, yet it is by means of the illumination of the white into the worlds of Creation, Formation and Making — which are the three colorings of the substances of the letters — that the vessels are made. Thus all the changes necessarily derive from the ten vessels of the *Sefirot* of Emanation, even though there are no vessels there when it is by itself for it is all white. Thus Emanation may be compared to the white of the book in relation to the letters and their combinations, for it is the illumination of Emanation to Creation, Formation and

Making that creates vessels in them.

You should now understand from what has just been explained how the *Tikkunei Zohar* can divide the world of Emanation into three aspects "He, His Vitality (*Hayyuhi*) and His Substance (*Garmuhi*)" although there is an absolute Unity there, and there is nothing whatsoever there of the aspect of created beings. For "He" refers to the divineness just as it is by itself; this is not understandable to us nor given to be understood, as has been explained previously with reference to all essences, even physical ones (see page 112). "His Substance" (*Garmuhi*) refers to the ten vessels of *Hokhmah* (wisdom) *Binah* (intelligence), *Tiferet* (beauty) and *Malkhut* (kingdom) which are to be found in the world of Emanation and which we compared to the white in a book of wisdom; it is impossible to conceive of even a number in the white part, for there is nothing that may make a number there for it is all white. However, not only do we give them a number but we also find all the millions of changes that become manifest in the Creation, Formation and Making — which constitute the aspect of the substance of the letters — are present at the outset in the vessels of *Hokhmah* (wisdom), *Binah* (intelligence), *Tiferet* (beauty) and *Malkhut* (kingdom) which are in the world of Emanation itself. However, this is to be understood as being just like the white which gives form to all of the letters in the book yet it does not itself possess any form, for the white becomes divided into thousands of forms even though it does not have any form itself. In a similar fashion the ten vessels that are in the Emanation become split into thousands of changes according to their illumination in the worlds of Creation, Formation and Making; which is just like the example we used of the conceptual plan that becomes implemented through the actual work of the building of the house. Thus all these changes that come about in the worlds of Creation, Formation and Making come only from the illumination of the vessels of the ten *Sefirot Hokhmah* (wisdom), *Binah* (intelligence), *Tiferet* (beauty) and *Malkhut* (kingdom) of Emanation; thus the myriads of changes that we find in the white come only from its relationship with those that receive in the worlds of Creation, Formation and Making. Whereas the Emanation itself is like the white which is by itself and which is not clothed in the ink of the letters, in which no number nor anything else whatsoever is to be found. We have thus explained the 'secret' (*sod*) of "His Substance" (*Garmuhi*) when in the form of vessels, yet by themselves they are an absolute unity just like "He". As for the word *Hayyuhi* ("His Vitality"), it refers to the light that is clothed in the white which consists of the vessels that we mentioned above. This light is also to be understood by us only in relation to the Souls (*Neshamot*) that receive from the Emanation, and not, heaven forbid, in its divineness as it is itself, for that is the 'secret' (*sod*) of "He" (*Iyhu*), as has been mentioned above. When the three worlds of Creation, Formation and Making ascend to the Emanation with the Souls (*Neshamot*) of human beings, the light that they receive there is refined to the aspect of the light of *Hokhmah* (wisdom) that is termed the light of the *Hayyah* (Living), and it is because of this aspect that we term the light there by the name of the light of *the Hayyah* (Living). Thus the statement of the *Tikkunei Zohar* that "He, His Vitality (*Hayyuhi*) and His Substance (*Garmuhi*) are One" is to be explained as meaning that all these aspects are described in reference to those that receive. Thus the aspect of *Garmuhi* ("His Substance") is the illumination of the vessels in the place of the Creation, Formation and Making that is beneath the "barrier" of the Emanation. The light of the Emanation never passes beneath the "barrier" of the Emanation but only the illumination of the vessels does. The aspect of *Hayyuhi* (His Vitality) is the illumination of the light of the Emanation itself, that is to say when the Creation, Formation and Making ascend to the Emanation. And *Iyhu* ("He") is the 'secret' (*sod*) of the divine essence which cannot be comprehended, as we mentioned previously. Thus the *Tikkunei Zohar* states that even though we, the receivers, can distinguish these three aspects of Emanation, however, this is only in their relationships with those that receive. From the aspect of the world of Emanation, as it is by itself, even *Garmuhi* (His Substance) is the aspect of *Iyhu* (He), that is to say, all are the divine essence. It is for this reason that it is impossible to comprehend the world of Emanation by itself, which is the 'secret' (*sod*) of the color white which cannot be comprehended by itself, therefore all that is there is absolute unity.

Thus when the Zohar describes the vessels *Hokhmah* (wisdom), *Binah* (intelligence), *Tiferet* (beauty) and *Malkhut* (kingdom) in the Emanation as growing larger or diminishing due to the actions of mankind, as it does for example in the passage (*Zohar*, 2:32) "Israel... gives might and strength to the Holy One blessed be He" which apparently refers to the divineness itself, this is not to be taken literally, heaven forbid, for no change at all is possible in the divineness, heaven forbid; as it is written "I *YHWH* have not changed" etc. Rather, since the Thought of Creation was to give pleasure to those created by Him we can therefore deduce that He possesses a "will to impart". Since we find in this world that the pleasure of someone who imparts grows when the number of those receiving from him multiplies, in fact, a person yearns to increase the number of those receiving, then from this aspect we can say that the "brains" (*Mohin*) grow in the Emanation when human beings are worthy of receiving the influence of the Emanation, or it can be said that, as it were, these human beings sustain Him. Furthermore, when the opposite occurs it also has an effect, that is to say when human beings are not fitting to receive His Emanation the "brains" (*Mohun*) contract, as it were, in a similar proportion, that is to say, there is none to receive from them.

In fact Emanation may be compared to a candle, for whether one lights thousands or millions of other lights from a candle or whether one does not light any other light at all from it, no change whatsoever will take place in the candle itself. Another example is that of Adam the first man, for whether there had come forth from him multitudes of sons that exist nowadays or even if he had not procreated at all, this fact would have effected no change at all on Adam himself. Similarly in the world of Emanation itself no change whatsoever occurs, heaven forbid, whether human beings of the lower world receive Emanation from it in great abundance or whether they do not receive anything, and thus the "growing" that has been mentioned takes place only in the human beings of the lower world.

However, since this is so, the question could well be asked, why does the Zohar describe all these changes as taking place in the world of Emanation? It should have explicitly stated that changes only take place in relation to those that receive in the worlds of Creation, Formation and Making. It should not have expounded so broadly on the world of Emanation that we should have to answer away all that it says. However, there is to be found in this a very powerful 'secret' (*sod*). It is the 'secret' (*sod*) of "And by the prophets I am represented in similitudes" (*Hosea*, 12:11). For in fact, it is the divine purpose that these images that occur only in the Souls (*Neshamot*) of those that receive, should appear to those souls (*Neshamot*) as if the Almighty Himself was a part of them, this is so to increase greatly the perception of the Souls (*Neshamot*). This can be compared to a father who artificially confines himself to show his beloved young son a sorrowful face and then a joyful face, even though he does not feel any sorrow or joy, but he only does this to activate his dear son and widen his understanding in order to play together. It is only after he grows up that he will understand that his father's actions were not real but he was only playing with him. The subject with which we are dealing is very similar; although all of these similitudes and changes only commence in the movement of the Souls (*Neshamot*) and it is in them that they finish, yet it is the divine purpose that they should appear to them as though they were taking place in the Almighty Himself. The Almighty does this so as to broaden and enlarge the perception of the Sousl (*Neshamot*) to their fullest capacity. This is contained in the Thought of Creation with the object of giving pleasure to His created beings.

You should not be surprised at this, for you will find similar instances of behavior in our own physical perception. Take, for example, our sense of sight with which we see in front of us a vast and beautiful world, yet in fact, we only see this inside ourselves, that is to say, in the back part of our brains where there is to be found a kind of photographic machine that draws pictures for us of everything that is seen by us, and there is nothing at all outside ourselves. Then the Almighty made for us, in addition to this, a kind of polished mirror in our brain that reflects to us everything that is visible there so that we may see it outside our brain and in front of our eyes. Yet although whatever we see outside of ourselves is not real, we still have much to be grateful for the Almighty's providence for having created this polished mirror in our brains which enables us to see and comprehend everything that is outside ourselves. For it is by means of this that we are able to reach a full and clear understanding of things, and we are able to measure things from inside and from outside; in fact, were it not for this process of seeing we should be lacking at least half of our knowledge. The same process is also true of the divine purpose in the case of the divine thoughts. For although these changes take place inside the Souls (*Neshamot*) that are receiving, yet they see them as all taking place in the Giver Himself, for it is only then, by these means, that the Souls can succeed in receiving all the ideas and all the pleasantness that are in the Thought of Creation. However, you may also deduce from this analogy that although we do in fact see everything in front of our eyes, yet every intelligent person knows clearly that everything that appears to us does so only inside our brains. The same is also true of the Souls (*Neshamot*), for although they see all these images in the Giver, yet they have no doubt whatsoever that all these occur only inside themselves and not at all in the Giver. Examine these words of mine well for I am unable at this juncture to broach this subject at greater length.

CHAPTER 8

THE ZOHAR ON IMAGERY

However, since these matters pertain to the mysteries of the world, I am very apprehensive in case the student should make mistakes in understanding them. I have therefore decided to take the further trouble of bringing the pure words of the Zohar itself on these matters and then of explaining them to the best of my ability.

The following is a passage from the Zohar in its pure and lucid style (*Bo*, page 42, side two on top of the page): "And if a person should ask, 'Is it not written "You saw no manner of image?" — which means, if a person should ask, is it not written in the Torah that "You saw no manner of image", how then can we attribute Names and *Sefirot* to the Almighty?

"He would then be answered 'I did surely behold an image, for is it not written, "And the image of the Lord will he (Moses) behold" (Num. 12:8)?' etc." — the explanation of this passage is that the answer will be that this image that I have seen is like that which is mentioned in the verse "And the image of the Lord will he (Moses) behold." This image is thus the *Sefirah* of *Malkhut* (kingdom) in which all the worlds and the Souls (*Neshamot*) have their roots. According to the 'secret' (*sod*), it is the root of all the vessels of those that receive from it and necessarily obtain vessels from it. It thus became refracted to them as an image about which it is written "And the image of the Lord will he behold."

"And even that image was a likeness of the Holy One, blessed be He, not in His own place, for that cannot be penetrated, but in the aspect of the King when He shows forth His power to rule over the whole of His creation, appearing to each of His creatures according to the capacity of each of them to see, envisage and imagine Him, and it is what is referred to in the verse (Hosea, 12:2), 'And through the prophets I am represented in images'." — The explanation of this passage is that this image, which we term the *Sefirah* of *Malkhut* (kingdom), does not occur in the place of the *Sefirah* itself as it is by itself, heaven forbid, but only when the light of the *Malkhut* (kingdom) descends and spreads out among His creatures does He then appear to every single one of them according to the sight and vision and imagination of each of them, that is to say, He appears only in the aspect of those that receive but by no means in the *Sefirah* of *Malkhut* (kingdom) as it is by itself, and this is the meaning of the verse "And through the prophets I am represented in images."

"And therefore He says: 'Although I appear to you in your own likenesses, to whom will you liken Me that I should be equal to him'?" — And for this reason the Holy One, blessed be He, says to them 'Although I appear to you in your own forms, that is to say in your vision and in your imagination, yet despite this to whom will you compare Me that I should be equal to him?'

"For before the Holy One blessed be He created any likeness or formed any form He was One without form or image." — The meaning of this passage is plain.

"Therefore it is forbidden to whoever has apprehended Him

as He is before creation, when He is outside of any form, to picture Him under any form or shape whatsoever, not even by the letter *Hei* nor by the letter *Yod*, nor even by the whole of His Holy Name, nor by any letter or sign whatsoever. This is the meaning of the verse 'For you saw no manner of image'." — And whoever comprehends Him before the level of Creation — which is the *Sefirah Binah* (intelligence) — when He is outside of any likeness, it is forbidden for that person to picture Him there by any form or likeness in the world, not by the letter *Hei* nor by the letter *Yod*, and it is even forbidden to call Him by the Name of Holy *YHWH*, or by any letter or sign whatsoever. This is the meaning of the verse "For you have not seen any similitude", that is to say that the verse "For you have not seen any similitude" refers to those who merit comprehending Him above the level of Creation, which is the level of *Sefirah Binah* (intelligence). For in the two *Sefirot Keter* (crown) and *Hokhmah* (wisdom) there is not to be found any aspect of form or image whatsoever, that is to say, of vessels or of boundaries (as we explained previously on page 118), for the vessels begin from the *Sefirah Binah* (intelligence) downwards. Therefore, all the allusions in the letters or in the signs or in the Holy Names only commence from the *Sefirah Binah* (intelligence) downwards; even then they do not occur in the place of the *Sefirot* themselves but only in those that are receiving, as we explained previously in the case of the *Sefirah Malkhut* (kingdom).

[At first sight there appears to be a contradiction here in the words of the Zohar, for it stated previously that it was only from the *Sefirah Malkhut* (kingdom) that the forms became extended to those that receive, for it stated "But He appeared in the aspect of a King ruling over His creation…" which is the 'secret' (*sod*) of the verse "And through the prophets I am represented in images". Yet here it states that it is from the Creation downwards, that is to say from the *Sefirah Binah* (intelligence) downwards, that the forms extend to those that receive. However, the explanation of this is that, in reality, forms and likenesses are only extended from the fourth aspect which is the *Sefirah Malkhut* (kingdom), and it is from *Malkhut* (kingdom) that the vessels extend into the place of those that receive, and nothing at all extends from the first nine *Sefirot* of *Keter* (crown), *Hokhmah* (wisdom), *Binah* (intelligence) and *Tiferet* (beauty). However, (as we explained in "The Introduction to the Wisdom of the Kabbalah") in the world of "correction" (*Tikun*) the attribute of *Rahamim* (compassion) was made a partner in the creation with the attribute of *Din* (judgement), which means that He raised the *Sefirah Malkhut* (kingdom) that is distinguished as the attribute of *Din* (judgement) and He brought it inside the *Sefirot Binah* (intelligence) that is distinguished as the attribute of *Rahamim* (compassion). Therefore, from that time onwards the vessels of *Malkhut* (kingdom) were rooted in the *Sefirah Binah* (intelligence), as, in fact, the Zohar states here. Thus the Zohar commences speaking of the real root of the images, which are the vessels, and states that they are in the *Sefirah Malkhut* (kingdom), then afterwards it states that they are in the Creation, which is the *Sefirah Binah* (intelligence), which has occured by force of the partnership which has taken place between the two attributes for the "correction" (*Tikun*) of the world. In a similar fashion our Sages of blessed memory stated "In the beginning the Holy One blessed be He created the world with the attribute of *Din* (judgement), when He saw that the world could not survive He brought in partnership with it the attribute of *Rahamim* (compassion)".

You should also know that the ten *Sefirot* of *Keter* (crown), *Hokhmah* (wisdom), *Binah* (intelligence), *Tiferet* (beauty)* and *Malkhut* (kingdom) are given many different names in the Zohar, according to their many different functions. Thus when they are given the names *Keter* (crown), *Atzilut* (Emanation), *Beriah* (Creation), *Yetzirah* (Formation) and *Asiyah* (Making) it will be their function to distinguish between the inner vessels that are termed *Keter* (crown) and *Atzilut* (Emanation), which are the *Sefirot Keter* (crown) and *Hokhmah* (wisdom), and between the hindmost vessels that are termed *Beriah* (Creation), *Yetzirah* (Formation) and *Asiyah* (Making), which are the *Sefirot Binah* (intelligence), *Tiferet* (beauty) and *Malkhut* (kingdom); this distinction came about due to the association of the attribute of *Din* (judgement) with the attribute of *Rahamim* (compassion). And because the Zohar wishes to allude to the association of the *Sefirah Malkhut* (kingdom) with the *Sefirah Binah* (intelligence) it calls the Sefirah *Binah* (intelligence) by the name *Beriah* (Creation). For before the association of these two attributes took place there was not to be found any form or likeness in the *Sefirah Binah* (intelligence), even in respect of those that receive, but these were to be found in *Malkhut* (kingdom) alone.]

The Zohar continues the passage we are quoting as follows: "But when He had created this form of the chariot of

---

* See p. 6, *Tiferet* includes six *Sefirot*.

supernal Man He descended there and was called *YHWH*, in order that they might know Him by His attributes and that He might be perceived in each attribute separately." — The explanation of this passage is that after He had made the form of the chariot of supernal Man, He descended and clothed Himself there and He became called by the form of the four letters *YHWH*, that is to say by the ten *Sefirot Keter* (crown), *Hokhmah* (wisdom), *Binah* (intelligence), *Tiferet* (beauty) and *Malkhut* (kingdom), for the upper tip of the *Yod* is *Keter* (crown), the *Yod* is *Hokhmah* (wisdom), the *Hei* is *Binah* (intelligence), the *Vav* is *Tiferet* (beauty) and the final *Hei* is *Malkhut* (kingdom). This process takes place so that the Almighty may be comprehended through His attributes, that is to say through the *Sefirot*, and through every single attribute that is His.

The Zohar is stating here that it is from the creation on-wards, that is to say from the *Sefirah Binah* (intelligence) — after it has been joined in partnership with the attribute of *Din* (judgement) which is the *Sefirah Malkhut* (kingdom) — that the likenesses and form extend to those that receive, namely the Souls (*Neshamah*), but these forms do not extend, heaven forbid, within the place of creation itself but only in the place of those that receive, as has been previously explained. The Zohar then proceeds to state that the Holy One blessed be He then made a form of the chariot of supernal Man and He descended and clothed Himself in the form of this man, by which it means to say that the form of man's body, which is made up of 613 vessels, extends from the vessels of the Soul (*Neshamah*), for the Soul (*Neshamah*) possesses 613 vessels consisting of 248 spiritual limbs and 365

spiritual sinews that may be divided into five sections according to the four letters of *YHWH* and the upper tip of the
Yod: — its head is the aspect of *Keter* (crown), from the
mouth to the chest is *Hokhmah* (wisdom), and from the chest
to the navel is *Binah* (intelligence), and from the navel until
the end of the two feet are the two *Sefirot Tiferet* (beauty)
and *Malkhut* (kingdom). Similarly the entire Torah is distinguished in the 'secret' (*sod*) of the *Partzuf* (countenance) of
man which is the 'secret' (*sod*) of the 248 positive *Mitzvot*
that correspond to the 248 limbs and of the 365 negative
Mitzvot that correspond to the 365 sinews. There are five
sections in it, which is the 'secret' (*sod*) of the five books
of the Torah, and it is this that is termed "The Form of
the chariot of supernal man" who is the Man of the creation, which is the *Sefirah Binah* (intelligence), for it is from
this *Sefirah* that these vessels begin to extend into the place
of the Souls (*Neshamot*). This man is termed the Supernal
Man because there are three aspects of man which are to be
found in the *Sefirot*, 'Man of Creation', 'Man of Formation'
and 'Man of Making', however, in the *Sefirot Keter* (crown)
and *Hokhmah* (wisdom) there is no likeness at all that could
possibly be called by any letter or sign, or by the four letters
of *YHWH*, as was explained previously. Since the Zohar is
speaking here of the world of Creation it is careful to use
the term "Supernal Man". You should constantly remember
the words of the Zohar that these likenesses do not occur in
the place of the *Sefirot Binah* (intelligence), *Tiferet* (beauty)
and *Malkhut* (kingdom), but only in the place of those that
receive. However, since these *Sefirot* impart to the vessels and
the "Garments" (*Levushim*) in order that they might know

Him by His attributes — so that the Souls (*Neshamot*) might comprehend Him by means of the light that extends to them in an attribute and in a restricted form through their 613 limbs — we therefore give these imparters the name of Man. However, they are merely the aspect of the color white as we explained previously (page 108).

You should also not find the following question difficult: Surely the four letters *YHWH* and the upper tip of the *Yod* constitute five vessels, as has been explained previously, for the vessels are always termed letters and they are the 'secret' (*sod*) of the five *Sefirot Keter* (crown), *Hokhmah* (wisdom), *Binah* (intelligence), *Tiferet* (beauty) and *Malkhut* (kingdom), as has been explained previously. Therefore, should it not be explicitly clear that there are also vessels in the *Sefirot Keter* (crown) and *Hokhmah* (wisdom) to which the upper tip of the *Yod* and the *Yod* itself of the *YHWH* allude? Thus, it appears that the *Sefirot Keter* (crown) and *Hokhmah* (wisdom) are considered vessels. However, the explanation of this question is that the Zohar speaks of the likenesses and of the attributes, which are the vessels, as beginning from the Creation downwards, that is to say in the three *Sefirot Binah* (intelligence), *Tiferet* (beauty) and *Malkhut* (kingdom) alone and not in the *Sefirot Keter* (crown) and *Hokhmah* (wisdom); this is the case for the aspect of the essence of the *Sefirot*. However, it is well known that all the *Sefirot* are made up of each other and each one contains all of the others, thus the ten *Sefirot Keter* (crown), *Hokhmah* (wisdom), *Binah* (intelligence), *Tiferet* (beauty) and *Malkhut* (kingdom) are to be found in the *Sefirah Keter* (crown), and similarly the *Sefirot Keter* (crown), *Hokhmah* (wisdom), *Binah* (intelligence), *Tiferet* (beauty) and *Malkhut* (kingdom) are to be found in the *Sefirah Hokhmah* (wisdom), and similarly the *Sefirot Keter* (crown), *Hokhmah* (wisdom), *Binah* (intelligence), *Tiferet* (beauty) and *Malkhut* (kingdom) are to be found in the *Sefirah Binah* (intelligence), and the same applies to the *Sefirah Tiferet* (beauty) and also to the *Sefirah Malkhut* (kingdom). Therefore, according to this, in each one of the five *Sefirot Keter* (crown), *Hokhmah* (wisdom), *Binah* (intelligence), *Tiferet* (beauty) and *Malkhut* (kingdom) there are to be found the three *Sefirot Binah* (intelligence), *Tiferet* (beauty) and *Malkhut* (kingdom) from which the vessels derive. By means of this you should understand that the upper tip of the *Yod*, which is the 'secret' (*sod*) of the vessels of the *Sefirah Keter* (crown), indicates the three *Sefirot Binah* (intelligence), *Tiferet* (beauty) and *Malkhut* that are contained in the *Sefirah Keter* (crown). And the *Yod* of *YHWH*, which is the vessel of the *Sefirah Hokhmah* (wisdom), indicates the *Sefirah Binah* (intelligence), *Tiferet* (beauty) and *Malkhut* (kingdom) that are contained in the *Sefirah Hokhmah* (wisdom). This occurs in such a way that the aspects of the *Sefirah Keter* (crown) and *Hokhmah* (wisdom) that are contained even in the *Sefirah* of *Binah* (intelligence) in both the *Tiferet* and *Malkhut* aspects of it, do not have any aspects of vessels whatsoever, whereas the aspects of *Binah* (intelligence), *Tiferet* (beauty) and *Malkhut* (kingdom) that are contained even in the *Sefirot Keter* (crown) and *Hokhmah* (wisdom) do have vessels connected to them. Thus from this aspect it would be true to say that there are five aspects of man, for the *Binah* (intelligence), *Tiferet* (beauty) and *Malkhut* (kingdom) that are in each of the five *Sefirot* influence through the 'secret' (*sod*) of the chariot of Man.

Therefore, there is a Man from the aspect of the *Sefirah Keter* (crown), and he is called Primordial Man (*Adam Kadmon*). And there is a Man from the aspect of the *Sefirah Hokhmah* (wisdom), and he is called Man of Emanation. And there is also a Man from the aspect of the *Sefirah Binah* (intelligence), and he is called Man of Creation. And there is also a Man from the aspect of the *Sefirah Tiferet* (beauty), and he is called Man of Formation. And there is also a Man from the aspect of the *Sefirah Malkhut* (kingdom), and he is called Man of Making.

The Zohar continues: "And He called Himself '*El, Elohim, Shaddai, Tzevaot* and *Ehyeh*' so that they might know Him through each of His attributes, and so that it may be made manifest how the world is sustained by mercy (*Hesed*) and judgement (*Gevurah*), according to the works of men." — And He called Himself by the Names '*El, Elohim, Shaddai, Tzevaot* and *Ehyeh*' so that they may know Him through each of His attributes. For the ten unerasable Names in the Torah are the 'secret' (*sod*) of the ten *Sefirot*. As it is written in the *Zohar* (*Vayikra*, 168): "The *Sefirah Keter* (crown) is called *EHYE*, and the *Sefirah Hokhmah* (wisdom) is called *Yah*. The *Sefirah Binah* (intelligence) is called *YHWH* with the vowels of *Elohim*, the *Sefirah Hesed* (mercy) is called *El*, the *Sefirah Gevurah* (judgement) is called *Elohim*, the *Sefirah Tiferet* (beauty) is called *YHWH*, the two *Sefirot Nezah* (lasting endurance) and *Hod* (majesty) are called *Tzevaot*, the *Sefirah Yesod* (foundation of the world) is called *El Hay* and the *Sefirah Malkhut* (kingdom) is called *Adonai*.

"For if His light was not shed over all of the creation, how then would they perceive Him? And how would the verse 'The whole earth is full of His glory' (*Isaiah* 6:3) be fulfilled?'' — This means that if His light did not spread over all creastures by means of His being clothed, as it were, in thse holy *Sefirot*, how then would His creatures come to know Him, and how then would the verse "the whole earth is full of His glory" be fulfilled? The Zohar is here attempting to explain that the divine purpose was to show to the Souls (*Neshamot*) that it is as though these changes in the *Sefirot* take place in Him Himself in order to give the Souls (*Neshamot*) room for a full and proper comprehension of Him, for then the verse in Isaiah "the whole earth is full of His glory" will be fulfilled, which is as we explained previously (page 134).

"Woe to the man who should presume to compare the Lord with any attribute, even with one of His own attributes, much less with any human form 'whose foundation is in the dust' (*Job*, 4:19), and who are ephemeral and worthless." — Consequently, woe to whoever compares the Almighty to an attribute, that is to say, one who says that the attribute is to be found in the Almighty as He is by Himself; even if he says this of one of the spiritual attributes in which He appears to the Souls (*Neshamot*). This is even more true for the physical attributes that pertain to human nature whose origins are dust and who are ephemeral and worthless. This is in fact just as we explained previously (page 136), that even though it is the divine purpose that the Souls (*Neshamot*) that receive should see these changes, that in fact take place in themselves, as taking place in the Giver, yet despite this, it should be clear to the Souls (*Neshamot*) that no change or attribute takes place in the Almighty Himself, heaven forbid, but it is merely the divine purpose that it should appear to them as though it does, according to the 'secret' (*sod*) of "And through the prophets I am represented in images" (Hosea, 12:11). However, if men should make this mistake then woe to them, for in an instant they will be cut off from the divine abundance; the same fate is of course in store for those fools who attribute to Him any characteristic of human beings who are made of flesh and blood and are ephemeral and worthless.

The student of Kabbalah would do well to study further the continuation of this passage in the Zohar that expounds the subject of the ten *Sefirot* and the three worlds of Creation, Formation and Making, however, this book is not the appropriate place to delve into these subjects at greater length.

Other RCK Publications of Interest to Readers of this Book

ENGLISH TEXTBOOKS

KABBALAH FOR THE LAYMEN
By Dr. Philip S. Gruberger

TEN LUMINOUS EMANATIONS
A textbook for beginners - from the writings of Rabbi Isaac Luria - by Rabbi Yehuda Ashlag - two volumes

GENERAL PRINCIPLES OF KABBALAH
A textbook for beginners - from the writings of Rabbi Moses C. Luzzatto - 1 volume

LIGHT OF REDEMPTION
By Rabbi Krakovsky. For beginners

THE POWER OF THE ALEPH BET
By Rabbi Shimon Ben Yohai. A dialogue of Creation between G-d and the Aleph Bet - 1 volume (May 1973)

HAKDAMOT
A collection of forward-looking introductions to the study of Kabbalah, by Rabbi Ashlag - first volume (Aug. 1973), second volume (Sept. 1973)

HEAVEN ON YOUR HEAD
Interpretations, Legends and Parables - by Dr. S. Z. Kahana

LEGENDS OF ISRAEL
Mystical insights and legends of Jewish Holy Days - by Dr. S. Z. Kahana

RCK is publishing a wide range of books in the field of KABBALAH. Originating primarily in Aramaic, a full series of publications in HEBREW have already been published with Present Emphasis on making available the KABBALAH Literature in ENGLISH.

Research Centre of Kabbalah
(established 1922)
P. O. Box 14168
Yeshivot Kol Yehuda Street
THE OLD CITY, JERUSALEM, ISRAEL

or

Research Centre of Kabbalah
200 Park Ave. Suite 303E
NEW YORK, N.Y. 10017